4-5-73

CHRIST PRESENT AND YET TO COME

The Priest and God's People at Prayer

CHRIST PRESENT AND YET TO COME

The Priest and God's People at Prayer

Joseph M. Champlin

ORBIS BOOKS
MARYKNOLL. NEW YORK

Dedication

To my brother priests in the Diocese of Syracuse
and our two shepherds
Bishops Walter A. Foery and David F. Cunningham.

Acknowledgments

I would like to thank the following individuals and publishers for permission to use copyrighted and personal material as noted below:

AMERICA—"Today's Priest—GP or More?" by Alexander Sigur reprinted with permission from *America*, March 7, 1970. All rights reserved. © 1970. America Press, Inc., 106 West 56th Street, New York, New York 10019.

—"Englishing the Liturgy" by G. B. Harrison reprinted with permission from *America*, May 9, 1970. All rights reserved. © 1970. America Press, Inc., 106 West 56th Street, New York, New York 10019.

BISHOPS' COMMITTEE ON THE LITURGY—*Newsletter*, January 1970; "The Place of Music in Eucharistic Celebrations"; *Newsletter*, December 1965; *The New Eucharistic Prayers and Prefaces*.

BRUSSELMAN, CHRISTIANE—"Prayer—the Need We Feel." A lecture at the Atlanta Liturgical Congress as transcribed and published in the April 1970 *Liturgy* of the Mobile Liturgical Commission.

DELANEY, DAVID—Letter to the editor of *America*, March 28, 1970.

GEOFFREY CHAPMAN LIMITED—*Sounds Effective* by Raymond Clarke. © 1969 Raymond Clarke.

I am also grateful for excerpts from other authors and publishers. In addition to those cited in the Notes, I would like to mention in particular:

CURRAN, CHARLES A. — "Personal Change Through Sermons," *Guide*, January 1964.

DOUBLEDAY AND COMPANY, INC. — Biblical quotations from *The Jerusalem Bible* © 1966.

GUILD PRESS, INC. — Quotations from conciliar texts are taken from *The Documents of Vatican II*, published by Guild Press, America Press, Association Press, and Herder and Herder, and © by America Press.

QUINN, JOHN J. — "The Lord's Supper and Forgiveness of Sin," *Worship*, May 1968.

Table of Contents

CHRIST PRESENT AND YET TO COME

The Priest and God's People at Prayer

INTRODUCTION

In the early fall of 1969 this writer began to give conferences for the clergy of a few dioceses on the then recently revised liturgy. These started in Davenport, Iowa, if I remember correctly, moved over to Winona, Minnesota, and shifted back east to Paterson, New Jersey. It was not a lecture series carefully planned by the national office or Secretariat of the Bishops' Committee on the Liturgy. In fact, such a development had not even been anticipated in the programming of activities for this period. The process, instead, simply involved independent invitations from individual bishops and their diocesan liturgical commissions to conduct full or half-day workshops for priests on the coming reforms in baptism, marriage, and the Mass.

These requests quickly multiplied and what originally amounted to several scattered appearances snowballed into a nation-wide speaking tour. With the efficient help of jet aircraft (and, in a few cases, the generous assistance of privately owned and operated single-engine Cessnas) I crisscrossed the country from October through March. These travels took me through

1

more than twenty states and into forty dioceses; brought me before some 11,000 priests and 15,000 religious or laity; supplied an exceptional opportunity to catch the current liturgical atmosphere of the United States and to learn about practical, pastoral efforts in a wide variety of parishes throughout the land. The things I said, the sights I saw, and the words I heard make up the substance of this book.

It was, naturally, an easy task. Clerical audiences, my priest readers would readily agree, are not at all hard to please. We drive willingly to conferences, arrive promptly on time, quickly come to attention. We listen attentively and are courteous, open, warmhearted. We are not disrespectful or hypercritical. We respond well, never grumble, never look at our watches, never walk out until dismissed. This is why every person who lectures at clergy meetings feels like Daniel as he walked into the lions' den.

My audiences, however, must have been fed well in advance. For the experience proved without exception both remarkable and most encouraging in each of those conferences. I found priests formerly wedded to traditional practices open to these new changes, and those already anxious for reform pleased and hopeful with the prospects. I saw older men talking more freely and eagerly with younger priests, and freshly ordained clerics viewing their senior confreres with respect and concern. (The three-day, fifty-man, retreat-style sessions at Grand Rapids were a perfect example of this.)

Pope Paul feels these liturgical revisions pave the way for a "new epoch" in the life of our Church. I must agree. They seem to contain great healing power, an ability to bring priests together again and the force once more to unite Christians around the altar. Such wild, Pollyanna forecasts may seem unreal in a world painfully split over questions of war, drugs, abortion, ecology, poverty, race, or whatever. But I merely report observations constantly positive from rural areas of the Crookston, Minnesota Diocese to vacation towns in the Orlando, Florida See, from Norwich, Connecticut, to Los Angeles, California.

The approach in the lectures and throughout this volume is pastoral. It views the liturgy as someting for the people. It seeks to aid priests in the difficult, delicate task of making Sunday worship in parishes full of meaning for persons in a modern world. It stresses spirit over law, common sense adaptations over uptight conformity, flexible needs of different congregations over standardized application of rigid rubrics.

Not that either Paul VI or the reformed Roman Missal speaks otherwise. The eight-chapter General Instruction sets in Article 6 both the tone of its directions and the path for tomorrow's worship.

> This instruction is intended to give general guidelines for celebrating the eucharist and also norms for each form of celebration. In accord with the Constitution on the Liturgy, each conference of bishops may establish additional norms for its territory because of the various traditions and character of the people, places, and communities.[1]

Pope Paul quite emphatically supports this officially flexible and legally adaptable liturgy. In an instruction on the renovated Order of Mass, he commented:

> The reform which is about to be brought into being is therefore a response to an authoritative mandate from the Church. It is an act of obedience. It is an act of coherence of the Church within herself. It is a step forward for her authentic tradition. It is a demonstration of fidelity and vitality, to which we all must give prompt assent.
>
> It is not an arbitrary act. It is not a transitory or optional experiment. It is a law. It has been thought out by authoritative experts of sacred Liturgy: it has been discussed and meditated upon for a long time. We shall do well to accept it with joyful interest and put it into practice punctually, unanimously and carefully.[2]

The author writes more from a pastoral background than from his post as a "Washington official who works for the bishops." He grew up and spent the first twenty-five years of his life in small, country towns. He knows well that in tiny parishes the pastor is lucky indeed if he has a competent organist, several good readers, a person who can lead the congregation in song.

In fact, such a priest often struggles to find a housekeeper or discover altar boys much less develop a complicated liturgical planning committee or parish program. This writer vividly recalls pre-Vatican II, summer vacation days in which he served simultaneously as sacristan (putting out wine and water, lighting candles, right side first, left side next, setting up altar), altar boy (vesting priest, reciting prayers at the foot of the altar, changing the missal, handling the cruets, ringing the bell), choir (singing from the *Liber Usualis* Latin Gregorian chant melodies to fulfill requirements for a high Mass stipend), and congregation (being the only communicant at that early hour). One does not easily forget such experiences.

A Cathedral church — large, downtown, inner-city — was his training ground for the first dozen years of priesthood. With five Masses daily; confessions morning, noon, and night; and all the sacramental or counseling work found in a parish at the city's heart, there were few pastoral situations which did not arise during that decade or more of work. Responsibility for several hospitals, a coroner's office, and many nursing homes as well as concern for a twelve-grade parochial school, extensive released-time CCD programs and continuous adult Inquiry Class added to his background. A wise pastor and talented, conscientious assistants contributed further to the education.

Even now his weekday office work is balanced by Saturday confessions, an occasional baptism or marriage, and Sunday Masses in a suburban Washington parish. The church is large, seats nearly 1,000 with parishioners white, well-educated, somewhat reserved because they work mainly in governmental posts and frequently must move to new locations. A sizeable percentage manifest conservative political and religious tendencies and they presently face what is for them a frightening school and community integration prospect. The priest can overcome that defensive reserve only through persistent effort and he needs in such a setting to speak with careful thought about racial issues.

I apologize for this biographical sketch; however, readers of a book purporting to speak from a pastoral point of view have a right to know the credentials of its author.

These pages should not be taken as an exhaustive manual on the new liturgy for pastoral theology classes. They contain limited abstract principles and concrete suggestions for the celebrant in this flexible liturgy now authorized. More certainly could and will be said in future days about the theory and practice of a priest's role. Still, the ideas in this volume did appear to assist priests with their understanding and acceptance of liturgical reforms when they were communicated by a living person. I hope these same concepts may prove helpful as they appear on the printed page.

Many remarks are intended primarily for priests. However, liturgy is no longer the clergy's prerogative. Good worship involves many persons fulfilling a diversity of functions. The General Instruction, Article 58, notes:

> Everyone in the eucharistic assembly has the right and duty to take his own part according to the diversity of orders and functions. Whether minister or layman, everyone should do that and only that which belongs to him, so that in the liturgy the Church may be seen as composed of various orders and ministries.[3]

Thus, the thoughts of this book should also appeal to those who exercise such a direct ministry and function in the liturgy or who are immediately involved in the preparation of liturgical celebrations.

A note about format. Priests (and presumably others as well) constantly feel the need to read but, for various reasons, find little time to do so. They snatch a few minutes at odd times and in strange places to skim an article or glance through a book. This volume has been broken into small sections and relatively short chapters with those habits precisely in mind.

I would like finally to express a word of gratitude to Mr. Philip Scharper, editor of Orbis Books, for his professional advice and personal encouragement, to Rev. Frederick R. McManus, director of the Secretariat, for ultimately making this volume possible, and to Mrs. Frances Pond, Mrs. Jean Petersen, and Mrs. Valerie Arthurs for their efficient and flawless typing of the manuscript.

PART I

THE CELEBRANT'S ATTITUDE
IN A FLEXIBLE LITURGY

Chapter 1

MASTER OF THE SITUATION

Seminaries a decade ago attempted to produce priests who were masters of what was required for valid and licit liturgical celebrations.

The rubrics were numerous, but precise; complicated, yet exact. We spent a good part of the deacon year learning "how" to offer Mass. Practically every room of a fourth-year theologian had its practice altar and there a future celebrant struggled each day with the fifty-plus signs of the cross, the many genuflections, the multiple bows. When he had achieved a more or less smooth combination of these components, the seminarian arranged for an appointment with his master of ceremonies or seminary rector.

On that occasion, quite tense and rather concerned, he went through his first "examination." The critic silently observed, took notes, and suggested areas for correction and improvement.

There was little room here for individuality. Instead, we strove for a perfect, ideal Mass — one in which every rubrical detail had been faithfully observed. Moreover, these official directives and authoritative commentaries covered the most minute gesture.

O'Connell's *The Celebration of Mass* served as *the* basis for those really concerned about liturgy. Other texts offered the fundamental material, but that volume plunged more deeply into the subject and contained everything anyone of prominence had written on the rubrics.

This excerpt from a section describing the approved manner in which one keeps one's hands joined before the breast at the specified times should refresh older minds and enlighten younger ones.

> The hands thus held are to be joined palm to palm, not merely fingers to fingers. The fingers are to be fully extended and *held together*, the right thumb over the left in the form of a cross. . . . When the hands are held thus joined the fingers should point slightly upwards, not towards the ground: the elbows are held close to the body. The hands are to be kept at the height of the breast, neither lower nor higher, and must not actually touch the vestment.[1]

In such an atmosphere the particular priest's personality and style formed a liability, not an asset. A model celebrant disappeared into the liturgical action. At Mass no one ought to be conscious that *he* was the priest. The congregation, instead, should observe only Christ working through him, should witness a meticulous execution of the sacred liturgy, should notice no difference between his celebration of the Eucharist and that of the cleric who followed him to the altar for the next service.

After Vatican II, the liturgical renewal, and our revised Order of Mass, these things seem almost unreal. Yet lest we mock our heritage and judge such preciseness absurd, it should be remembered that reverence for worship and respect for the priest ran high in those days. People felt this was a sacred event, these were holy actions, and the priest who performed them acted as God's specially anointed instrument. Such deeds channelled grace almost automatically, "ex opere operato," to man through the consecrated hands and lips of this unique, set-aside individual. If the Lord's minister did the right thing and uttered the correct words, then Jesus became present in our midst. The priest, according to this approach, naturally occupied a vital post and deserved special recognition.

The liturgical movement brought about a change in that attitude. Concern shifted from the priest in the sanctuary and at the altar to the person beyond the communion railing and in the pews. Without denying the truth or value of this efficacious, grace-conveying liturgy, we came to understand a little more clearly that faith, devotion, and participation upon the part of a congregation plays an equally indispensable role.

Saint Pius X said it all at the turn of the century. To acquire the true Christian spirit, he insisted, we must go to "its first and indispensable source, namely, active participation in the most sacred mysteries and in the public and solemn prayer of the Church."[2] This message has been restated, underscored, quoted, developed, interpreted by popes and bishops and liturgists constantly since 1903. However, it can be reduced to an essentially simple principle: Get the congregation actively to participate with faith and love in the liturgy. The Fathers at Vatican II spelled out in their Liturgy Constitution what that means from a practical point of view

> By way of promoting active participation, the people should be encouraged to take part by means of acclamations, responses, psalmody, antiphons, and songs, as well as by actions, gestures and bodily attitudes. And at the proper times all should observe a reverent silence.[3]

In recent years we have experienced moderate success with these efforts at active participation. Priests now normally face the people, address them in their own language, and hear a response. Congregational singing is more common in parishes even though efforts to promote it limp along with uneven results dependent upon a host of factors. Educational programs on the liturgy generally emphasize those faith and love aspects essential for any meaningful worship.

Still, the celebrant's function has, in a subtle way, been de-emphasized through this concentration on congregational involement. He is not so significant anymore; those "out there" are the ones to be turned on. We need dialogue homilies, swinging music, and imaginative offertory processions. We need theme Masses, lay lectors, and full-time directors of music. We need liturgy committees in every community to plan each celebration and help to prepare the priest for his task.

No one truly can question, of course, the necessity and advantage of this directional change in our approach to liturgical matters. Unless the entire People of God share in a service it hardly deserves the title of public prayer or official worship. At the same time, such a motion away from preoccupation with rubrics toward concern for participation has apparently minimized the priest's part.

I wonder if, with this new and flexible liturgy, we are not now or at least will soon experience a trend bringing us, as it were, full circle. I do not mean a reversion to excessive "valid and licit" considerations of the past nor an abandonment of the present regard for the congregation. What I have in mind is the role of the celebrant who puts it all together; who actually assembles a diversity of people and parts into one united, moving act of worship; who by his own presence, faith, and love truly leads them in prayer. In a word, to take Father Gerard T. Broccolo's description, "the celebrant at this reformed Mass will serve as master, not merely of the rubrics, but of the total situation."[4]

Number 313 of the General Instruction to the Roman Missal supports this assertion and delineates the celebrant's function:

> The pastoral effectiveness of a celebration depends in great measure on choosing readings, prayers, and songs which correspond to the needs, spiritual preparation, and attitude of the participants. This will be achieved by an intelligent use of the options which are described below.
>
> In planning the celebration, the priest should consider the spiritual good of the assembly rather than his own desires. The choice of texts is to be made in consultation with the ministers and others who have a function in the celebration, including the faithful.

> Since a variety of options is provided, it is necessary for the deacon, readers, cantors, commentators, and choir to know beforehand the texts for which they are responsible, so that nothing will upset the celebration. This careful planning will help dispose the people to take their part in the eucharist.[5]

This master of the situation function, however, extends beyond a harmonious advance planning of the liturgy into the actual celebration of worship. The priest at the altar or pulpit or baptismal font must also lead, integrate, preside over the service. And he needs to do so with a sound awareness of what should be accomplished, with a belief in its worth, and with a desire fully to involve the people present.

No one anticipates a reversal to older days or rubricism. The Liturgy Constitution in Article 11 sealed that escape hatch. "Pastors of souls must therefore realize that, when the liturgy is celebrated, more is required than the mere observance of the laws governing valid and licit celebrations. It is their duty also to ensure that the faithful take part knowingly, actively, and fruitfully."[6]

But no priest, on the other hand, should feel his position in worship is of little consequence. Quite the contrary. The Council Fathers require something more, not less, of the celebrant. They, and the Congregation for Divine Worship following their guidelines, make him the leader of liturgy and demand an attitudinal change on his part for a successful discharge of this added role.

The chapters of Part I which follow will describe some aspects of that adjustment in attitude and give practical illustrations of this leadership role in action.

Chapter 2

MAN OF PRAYER

Most parish priests I know feel quite fatigued by the middle of Sunday afternoon. Binating or trinating, greeting the people before and after each service, preaching, filling out Mass cards, taking care of baptisms and recording the details, supervising CCD classes — these activities take their toll. Part of the cause for this weariness is the understandably energy-consuming task as leader of worship. To stand before several hundred or a thousand people for forty-five minutes, to speak with conviction, to pray with meaning necessarily causes a certain amount of creative tension and inner nervousness. To be drained afterwards could almost be considered a sign that the duty was seriously undertaken and conscientiously discharged.

This nervous, intense atmosphere, however, renders personal, internal prayer difficult for the celebrant. He tends to think of his time at the altar as a work period, even if the labor is sacred and the function rewarding. I would think few priests regard Sunday Mass as the occasion to step aside, reflect, put life into perspective. Such subjective reflections come before or after or at some other moment during the day.

That emphasis of former days on correct rubrical procedures further heightened this pressure and concern. There was only one text to be followed, one way to perform a certain action. Ordination imposed an obligation upon the priest to know what the *Ordo* directed for a given day and obey its precise notations exactly, to master the many rubrics and observe them carefully. Reverence in the sanctuary and correctness about the altar were perhaps the two dominant criteria for excellence on the part of a cleric.

The revised Order of Mass encourages this same reverence, but hopes it will take on a more joyful, less somber tone. The General Instruction seeks a proper, correct Eucharistic celebration, but wishes it to assume a more natural, relaxed character.

The latter document offers a total picture of the priest as leader of worship:

> A presbyter as celebrant also presides over the assembly in the person of Christ, leads it in prayer, proclaims the message of salvation, leads the people in offering sacrifice through Christ in the Spirit to the Father, and shares with them the bread of eternal life. At the eucharist he should serve God and the people with dignity and humility. By his actions and by his proclamation of the word he should impress upon the faithful the living presence of Christ.[1]

The rubrics in Chapter IV of the same text and in the actual Order of Mass enable celebrants to lead a congregation in prayer much more easily and naturally. Thus, to illustrate, instead of minute regulations for joined or extended hands the text simply directs, "Afterwards the priest, with hands joined, sings or says . . . ," and "Then the priest extends his hands and sings or says the opening prayer. . . ."[2]

These more liberal rules will not eliminate the almost necessary tension or nervousness which accompanies a celebrant's role as "performer" (in the good sense of the term). But they should reduce preoccupation with minor matters and facilitate concentration on the more central aspects of each service. At greater ease and under less pressure the priest may even come to a point in which he can not only lead the others officially in prayer but also reflect personally in his heart, particularly during moments of silence specified by the new rite.

We would call those several opportunities for quiet reflection in the reformed Mass periods of disciplined silence. Vatican legislation no longer permits "silent" celebrations, but it does mandate occasional silence within worship. The priest who has become sufficiently comfortable in his function around the sanctuary may then discover that these pauses cease to seem wasted, awkward intervals and begin to assume the nature of personal, intimate minutes with God.

To illustrate:

1. *During the penitential service*: Disciplined silence means a turning on and off of our thoughts. Americans are not really accustomed to this. It will take time for celebrant and congregation to develop a versatility in such a practice. The words, "Let us call to mind our sins," refer to the priest as well as to others present. If he really ponders his past hours or days or weeks and his own failures of commission or omission, the time will neither drag nor appear pointless. And those in the pews quickly will catch the message from his example alone.

2. *Before the opening Communion prayer*: The "Let us pray" suggests that "Priest and people pray silently for a while." In a moment, he will gather all their private, individual, unspoken petitions and present them to the Father through the Son in the Spirit. But now he, with them, reflects and prays for himself, for the parish, for the Church, the community, the nation, and the world. The celebrant who attempts this will quickly recognize the necessity for prolonging that silent pause. It takes us a few seconds simply to get thoughts organized much less move on to conversation with Christ or meditation on man's condition. Too brief a period of silence proves frustrating and fruitless.

3. *After the biblical readings and homily*: Article 23 of the General Instruction says, "At the conclusion of a reading or homily, each one meditates briefly on what he has heard." The priest who in fact does pray as a celebrant listens attentively to the readings and reflects earnestly on them. His eyes, expres-

sion, and posture will quickly reveal either an attitude of meditative prayer, or a roving curiosity or an impatient anxiety to get on with the service.

4. *At thanksgiving after Communion*: This same article of the General Instruction suggests the worshiper silently "after communion praises God in his heart and prays." The celebrant should lead the way in such a thanksgiving and not suggest that his congregation do so while he attends to the details of cleaning chalice and plate.

5. *In the remembrance for the living and the dead*: The pause explicitly indicated in Eucharistic Prayer I (and possibly at the appropriate spot in the intercessions of the other three formulas) for mention of specific persons alive and deceased also gives the celebrant an opportunity to recall the names of his own relatives, friends, and associates. In similar fashion a prayerful use of that moment without any effort or affectation on his part quietly communicates a message to the faithful who join him for this Eucharist.

The celebrant also is praying, however, when he says or sings those parts assigned him, when he listens to the reader, when he unites with all in common words like the Lord's Prayer. There are no clean, neat, easy directions on how one achieves such an ideal. But basically each priest must appreciate what this is all about, understand the meaning of the phrases uttered, and possess a prayerful attitude as he performs his tasks.

The present official liturgy contains little provision for spontaneous prayer on the part of priest or congregation. Nevertheless, the priest adept at creative, on-the-spot leadership might wish to use the introduction and conclusion to the general intercessions or prayer of the faithful for some type of more personal worship. The invitation and concluding prayer (prepared in idea if not in script) could then manifest some of his inner convictions and thoughts, be tied in with the homily and theme of the celebration, and impart a feeling of honesty and earnestness. Extremes should be avoided and care taken lest spontaneity slip into sloppiness or authenticity descend into sentimentalism.

All these remarks presuppose, on the priest's part, some sort of private, personal prayer beyond formal, official worship. One may question the validity of, for example, the Divine Office, the rosary, or structured meditation, but I think he who scoffs at moments set aside for reflection on God, himself, and the world is heading for disaster in his ministry and ineffectiveness as a celebrant.

Father Andrew Greeley concurs. In his *New Horizons for the Priesthood* he observes, "For this reason, if the priest is to be the man to whom others turn, the man who is a relational man par excellence, the man whose life and ministry symbolizes unity among the Christian people, he must be a praying man."[3]

He expands this concept and explains why such prayer is necessary for the priest in the following excerpt:

> But the committed Christian believing in the good news of the Lord Jesus, believing in the Resurrection, believing in the promise of the return, has no desire to cut himself off from liturgical unity with the world and with the human community in which he is immersed. He prays in his relationship with the world, with men, with himself and with God. He knows that peace flows from an increased understanding of the unities in which he is immersed and also from an increased emotional involvement in these unities. He prays publicly because public prayer is a celebration of unity, and he reflects privately because he knows that in these private reflections he comes to understand profoundly the impact of these unities of his life.[4]

In summary, therefore, the priest who comes across as a model man of prayer in the liturgy needs an element of self-confidence or stage presence before his congregation, a fundamental comfortableness in front of crowds, together with the attitude and spirit of a man who prays. Unfortunately, the former generally comes in greater or less degree as a gift from God and from one's parents although experience, familiarity, hard work, and grace can do wonders when a little talent and a lot of good will are present.

Desirable though such human traits may be in the ideal celebrant, they end up shallow, useless, even hypocritical, without the accompanying spirit of prayerfulness. On the other hand, the priest bereft of these gifts but who truly cares; who loves God, the Eucharist, and his people; who prays unceasingly; and who does his fumbling best at the altar will touch hearts and move people. The faithful know. They see through us. They understand when a man prays, even if they do wish he were more confident and less afraid in the sanctuary.

The basis for prayer and the motive prompting a man to pray ultimately is faith. We will talk about that in this next chapter.

Chapter 3

FAITH AND COMMITMENT

Priestly spirituality before 1950 relied heavily on the monastic concept of prayer, life, and worship. It generally stressed withdrawal from this world in the tradition of Thomas a Kempis and his *The Imitation of Christ*. It regarded God as the Supreme Being who deserved our unquestioning obedience and humble acknowledgment. Private prayer, the Divine Office, Mass itself, according to this approach, sent human acts of faith, hope, love, adoration, petition, thanksgiving, and reparation upwards to the Divinity. Personal feelings did not count much when it came to evaluating the validity of a particular prayer form; the action itself spoke for us. Nor was there any anxious desire or felt need to relate constantly what we did in church or on our knees to the noisy and demanding life swirling around us.

The dangers attendant upon such an attitude are basically mechanism (praise for the routine repetition of acts without corresponding emphasis on the faith and love elements which should motivate these deeds); irrelevance (failure to bring worship and the world together, thus creating a sterile and artificial liturgy divorced from life); and superstition (a view of instrumental words, actions, or persons as causes of grace apart from the God who gives *through* these media and independent of those sentiments in each recipient's heart which determine a sacrament's effectiveness).

We have shifted away from that trend in recent years. Concentration today is more on the individual person, upon his feelings, upon the way he reacts to a particular sacrament or a special celebration. Unless he believes, hopes, or loves, we tend to think the service limps or even lacks validity. The idea that God should be adored and worshiped regardless of my dispositions today or at this moment holds little power in the minds of some. The breviary means nothing to you? Drop it, replace it with scriptural readings, contemporary literature, or even the late show on television. You don't feel able psychologically or emotionally to celebrate the Eucharist this morning? Forget it, try again tomorrow or the next day.

Certain obvious pitfalls exist here also. We might categorize them as selfishness (overlooking the priest as a servant of the people, one who has been commissioned to care for their spiritual needs regardless of personal weariness, boredom, or inconvenience); excessive humanism (omitting the faith and the divine, transcendent aspects of prayer and liturgy in an overconcern for humanly attractive experiences); and activism (operating totally on an action-centered schedule, finding God only in people, never withdrawing, as Greeley has suggested, for a few moments of contact with the Lord within one's inner self to extablish a root unity and some ultimate priorities).

This is a complicated question indeed. For this writer, however, the solution, as usual, remains somewhere in the center. Any leader of worship standing at the altar must be a bridge between extremes, a master of the situation, a man of prayer, a person of faith. It is his role to foster humanly attractive worship services which will inspire the people's faith. Nevertheless, it is his function also to point out that given the finite and complex condition of man, liturgy doesn't always move us, doesn't always give us an emotional uplift, doesn't always make us feel better. He should be a man for others, yes, but the priest likewise must be a believer in the Other. He needs to communicate a sense of the infinite, a belief in a supreme, creating, loving Lord who deserves our love, our adoration, our acknowledgment of dependence. Quite simply, the celebrant, while working for meaningful liturgies, must also manifest faith in a God who should be honored by public and private prayer even when humanly speaking we do not seem quite up to it.

There is, therefore, an interrelation between the faith element in liturgy and the human experience of those who worship. In point of fact, the more humanly attractive the service, the better public prayer it will be. For example, an organist who drags resurrection hymns at funereal pace casts a pall over the entire congregation. Little Easter joy will fill *that* church during the spring season. Similarly, the guitar group which insists on singing all two dozen verses of their favorite tune will drive those in the pews up the church wall. Tired feet, weary voices, and irritated ears may mean merit for the suffering parishioner, but they effectively cancel out satisfying participation by the people.

In November 1967, the Bishops' Committee on the Liturgy issued a statement prepared by their Music Advisory Board on "The Place of Music in Eucharistic Celebrations" which underscores this point: "The primary goal of all celebration is to make a humanly attractive experience." However, lest one interpret an isolated statement out of context, the document goes on to explain why that *is* the primary goal of public worship: "From this it is clear that the manner in which the Church celebrates the liturgy has an effect on the faith of men. Good celebrations foster and nourish faith. Poor celebrations weaken and destroy faith."

A section, "The Theology of Celebration," in that statement of the Bishops' Committee, represents probably the clearest and most succinct expression of these faith and liturgy concepts in print today:

> We are Christians because through the Christian community we have met Jesus Christ, heard his word of invitation, and responded to him in faith. We assemble together at Mass in order to speak our faith over again in community and, by speaking it, to renew and deepen it. We do not

come together to meet Christ as if he were absent from the rest of our lives. We come together to deepen our awareness of, and commitment to, the action of his Spirit in the whole of our lives at every moment. We come together to acknowledge the work of the Spirit in us, to offer thanks, to celebrate.

People in love make signs of love and celebrate their love for the dual purpose of expressing and deepening that love. We too must express in signs our faith in Christ and each other, our love for Christ and for each other, or they will die. We need to celebrate.

We may not feel like celebrating on this or that Sunday, even though we are called by the Church's law to do so. Our faith does not always permeate our feelings. But this is the function of signs in the Church: to give bodily expression to faith, to transform our fragile awareness of Christ's presence in the dark of our daily isolation into a joyful, integral experience of his liberating action in the solidarity of the celebrating community.[1]

The faith mentioned here still remains somewhat general. More specifically, what does or should the celebrant as a man of faith believe in and wish to share with those who join him for worship? We give a simple, but wide-ranging answer: God, Christ, the Church, Jesus' good news of salvation.

The priest, if he is to radiate this faith fundamental to good liturgy, needs to believe that God is, and cares for us. For him the Lord Jesus, his paschal mystery of coming, dying, rising, returning, his gospel message is real and personal. Salvation history to such a celebrant is not a technical term from an academic course in biblical theology, but a constant here and now event. He believes the Creator's saving action in our world has a past, present, and future dimension. What God did once for all in Christ at the Last Supper, on Calvary, during Easter, he continues to accomplish in the Eucharist, through sacraments and by his grace for persons of the current age.

The Church for this type of priest serves as a symbol of Jesus present and active in the world — teaching men to love the Father and their fellowman, inspiring them to follow the beatitudes, instructing us about the root goodness of creation. That Church gives hope to every individual, confidence that the kingdom ful-filling all our longings will come soon even while it shows us Christ's reign already is with us in incomplete form at this very instant. The celebrant filled with belief in an already, but not yet kingdom of heaven links his joyful, trusting expectation for the future with an energetic, don't-waste-a-second, be-open-to-every-living-sound attitude for the present.

How, in practical terms, Christ and his kingdom does become present to us through prayer and a worship permeated with faith will be the topic of our next chapter.

Chapter 4

THE PRESENCE OF CHRIST

Article 7 of the Constitution on the Sacred Liturgy in many ways forms something of a doctrinal base for everything which follows in the conciliar decree. The reforms projected, the guidelines recommended, even the ideals sketched rest upon this article for foundation. Thus it establishes theological backing for the remark: "From this it follows that every liturgical celebration, because it is an action of Christ the priest and of His Body the Church, is a sacred action surpassing all others. No other action of the Church can match its claim to efficacy, nor equal the degree of it."[1]

So, too, the faith and commitment required in celebrants of a revised, flexible liturgy centers on the truth that Christ is present in his Church's prayer and worship. We quote the pregnant words of this article's initial sentence: "To accomplish so great a work, Christ is always present in His Church, especially in her liturgical celebrations."

This multifaceted presence of Christ contains many pragmatic implications and I hope to draw them out through a point by point examination of Section 7.

"He is present, finally, when the Church prays and sings, for He promised: 'Where two or three are gathered together for my sake, there am I in the midst of them' (Mt. 18:20)."

The priest who really believes this and puts it into practice will take a slightly different approach to grace before meals, invocations at banquets, and informal prayer in meetings. No one, for example, may criticize the standard formula, "Bless us, O Lord . . . ," but some might object to the perfunctory manner in which we occasionally recite it. Others will suggest that we prepare something in advance, or ponder over it earlier during a period of prayer or, if we have developed a competence for this through experience, spontaneously compose a blessing at the moment. The more personal and from one's heart it is, the more our faith in God's presence will shine through this simple, brief prayer beginning a family meal, diocesan congress, or public function. If we really believe Christ is present when we pray together, it affects the way we act during such prayer.

In my seminary days any student who suggested getting together for common, informal prayer received the silent, question-mark kind of treatment. At that time we just didn't seem to have any wish to unveil secret thoughts and inner aspirations for others to see. The pattern appears different today. Sensitivity programs, dialogue homilies, and weekend encounters have taught seminarians the need and developed in them the desire for a sharing of common sorrows and joys, mutual hopes and failures. These things naturally carry over into the priesthood and one discovers every now and then rectories in which the clergy gather for prayer sessions.

At a suburban parish in the Paterson, New Jersey Diocese, the pastor and his three associates assemble each Monday afternoon before dinner for a half hour of reflection. They begin with a joint recitation of None. One of the priests then reads a brief passage on some subject of current concern. During the balance of the thirty minutes, they meditate or comment in a prayerful spirit and with an awareness of the Lord's presence in their midst. Such sessions contain built-in power to dissolve bitterness which may have arisen over disagreements about parochial policy. Priests who pray together also tend to live more happily together. Their Christian love for each other and the common faith which prompts that sensitive care will not go unobserved by parishioners.

People who resent singing during Communion time and judge this an unwarranted invasion of their privacy or an unwanted interruption of their personal conversation with the Lord in the Eucharist might be more amenable to a congregational song if they understood clearly that Christ is also really present when the "Church prays and sings."

"He is present in His word, since it is He Himself who speaks when the holy Scriptures are read in the church."

The leader of worship who truly believes that Christ is present in the Bible should find that this faith carries over into his actions. That kind of belief would prompt him to train lectors carefully, arrange scriptural prayer services for special occasions, and read the sacred text daily himself. It establishes a certain priority of values in a man's heart and leads him to insist that care and reverence characterize any person or ceremony employing the inspired Word of God.

A visitor to Most Holy Rosary Church in Lowellville, Ohio, notes immediately upon entering the vestibule a stand with an open Bible resting upon it. An overhead spotlight draws one's eye to the text and silently says: God is here, in this book, within these pages.

Those who stop at St. Augustine's Cathedral in Tucson, Arizona, for the Sunday morning Mass will see two laymen marching solemnly in the entrance procession, one with a richly ornamented Book of Gospels and the other with an equally decorated lectionary, held high above their heads. The former is placed upright on the altar and the other is taken to the lectern. The solemnity, the elegant binding, the placement in a position of prominence—these gestures also speak in quiet terms about the Lord's presence in Holy Writ.

This reformed lectionary for Mass opens up the treasures of the Bible more richly for Sunday and weekday use. In addition,

the General Instruction to the Roman Missal provides those responsible for worship the freedom and opportunity to select other
readings when circumstances dictate, as long as they can be
found in the approved lectionary itself. The priest who consis-
tently reads and studies Sacred Scripture, who realizes the possibilities for use of the Bible within present legislation and takes
advantage of them, who spends time in preparing a homily for
the next day's Eucharist, will be offering his people what a-
mounts to an ongoing course in biblical theology. The celebrant's faith in Christ present through his word will, again,
overflow into the hearts of parishioners and strengthen their
belief in the uniqueness of God's presence in the Bible.

   *"By His power He is present in the sacraments, so that when a
man baptizes it is really Christ Himself who baptizes."*

   Back in the early fifties, Father A. M. Roguet, a French
Dominican, wrote *Christ Acts through the Sacraments*.[2] Still a
sound volume and available in paperback, it captures the deeper
meaning and further ramifications of what Vatican II Fathers
were saying in this sentence. Thus, when I hear confessions,
Christ hears through me; when I baptize, it is really Christ himself who baptizes; when I anoint someone, it is truly Christ who
acts in this sacrament.
   These are powerful words and should influence the way in
which we priests discharge a sacramental ministry. But repetition, routine, and rush can cause us to grow shoddy in our
habits.
   It is not easy to remember that Christ actually is baptizing
when you have six screaming infants on a sticky summer afternoon with parents and sponsors more interested in the parties
which follow than in the ceremony at hand. It is not easy to
keep in mind that Christ really sits with you in a cramped confessional box after three straight hours on a Holy Saturday afternoon, especially when the penitents seek only a mechanical
fulfillment of their annual obligation or a fresh supply of grace to
cover the same laundry list of sins confessed two weeks earlier.
It is not easy to recall that Christ heals and forgives when you

get up at 2:00 A.M., travel to a nursing home, and anoint a ninety-year-old man, unknown to you, unconscious, wasting away, without friends or relatives.

But the fact remains and the truth persists: it is really Christ himself who acts.

"He is present. . . especially under the Eucharistic species."

The recently renovated Cathedral in Springfield, Massachusetts, features the Blessed Sacrament in a side chapel connected with, but distinct from, the main sanctuary. Despite removal of the tabernacle from its customary center-of-the-church location, there seems no diminution of respect nor lessening of devotion to the Real Presence under the Eucharistic species. Quite the contrary. The architect/artist has designed special lighting and a colorful mosaic to attract attention toward this spot whenever no liturgical actions are in progress at the central altar.

Nor have the laity forgotten that Christ is present in a real, unique, even if mysterious, way within the tabernacle. They stop for visits; kneel for a prayer; sit and gaze and sort out the enigmas or insolubles of their own lives; weigh imponderables from a different view and in the divine presence. It is good when priests do the same.

I remember well my elderly pastor, clothed in overalls and bathed in sweat after mowing the lawn of his small, rural parish, kneeling for night prayers at the communion rail of his darkened church. I recall also during my summer seminary days as a salesman stopping regularly at a suburban church and invariably finding the pastor near the tabernacle for a late afternoon visit. Those sights inspired me then, and I think that, despite our greater sophistication and action-oriented patterns of prayer, they continue to move people today.

In any event, the priest who firmly believes in Jesus' eucharistic presence will react accordingly. We would expect a man like this to allocate daily periods of prayer before the Blessed Sacrament, to keep the sanctuary decorated but clean and uncluttered, to exhibit always a comfortable reverence about the church, yet on guard lest familiarity breed casualness.

We would also look for this type of celebrant to display special concern for his people during the distribution of Holy Communion within or outside of Mass. Believing that moment to be their individual, faith-filled contact with the Eucharistic Lord, he would take pains to make the occasion as effective as possible. Such diligence extends from arranging for an ample number of ministers (including laymen or laywomen, if necessary), to planning appropriate hymns, to distributing hosts for each communicant by name.

The priest's (or other minister's) "The Body of Christ," represents an invitation; the recipient's "Amen," a response. The true connotation of the "Amen" at Communion time may be obscure for contemporary man; but basically it embraces the idea of "I believe, I trust, I love the Lord, I wish to receive him." Many celebrants today feel mention of the person's name with this invitation, where possible, can help clarify and emphasize the true meaning of an individual's "Amen."

One celebrant who has followed that procedure at parish Masses quotes this letter in support of his action. "I have been meaning to tell you how delighted Eddie was on Christmas Eve when at Holy Communion you said, 'Edward, the Body of Christ.' He has never been to a Mass before where this was done and he literally floated out of the church that night."

"He is present in the sacrifice of the Mass, not only in the person of His minister, 'the same one now offering, through the ministry of priests, who formerly offered himself on the cross,' but especially under the Eucharistic species."

The other presences of Christ we have mentioned are unquestionably real and significant, but they ultimately lead to or flow from his presence in the Eucharist. Hans Küng maintains this in his monumental study, *The Church.*

> Christ is present in the entire life of the Church. But Christ is above all present and active in the *worship of the congregation* to which he called us in his Gospel, and into which we were taken up in baptism, in which we celebrate the Lord's Supper and from which we are sent again to our work of service in the world.[3]

It is this active presence of Christ in Eucharistic celebrations which fills churches for daily Mass in Ireland, which sustained prisoners in World War II concentration camps, and which today draws hundreds of college students to Newman centers on college campuses. It is here that the Lord Jesus becomes preeminently present; it is here that the Church primarily happens or occurs; it is here that the priesthood has its fullest and finest meaning.

An awareness of these things simply has to influence the style of a priest whether he is listening in silence at the presidential chair or proclaiming a preface at the altar of sacrifice.

However, to believe and be committed to Christ's presence in common prayer, in the Bible, in the tabernacle, in the sacraments, in the Mass presupposes a definite faith in and commitment to the priesthood, and to liturgical worship. We now move on to discuss those areas of concern.

Chapter 5

SHEPHERD, PREACHER, CELEBRANT

Msgr. Alexander O. Sigur is the extremely talented and dynamic pastor of St. Genevieve Church in Lafayette, Louisiana. He can fly an airplane, write scholarly articles, and deliver profound lectures. Formerly National Newman Club Chaplain, Msgr. Sigur used a review of Corpus Publication's new book, *Hyphenated Priests*, as his springboard to discuss the current question of priestly identity.

The article, "Today's Priest — GP or More?," ran in *America* magazine on March 7, 1970, and raised serious doubts about the satisfying nature of a strictly "pastoral" ministry. To quote him:

> Many priest are bored. They yearn for more than general practice. They want to study, to learn, to serve with special skills and talents. They crave expertise at times, not for remuneration primarily (Paul as tanner found comfort and sustenance in professional capacity) but for fulfillment of what they are capable, in service of the Church. . . .
>
> A priest can hardly be held in this age to a full work-day or week of tasks clearly definable as "priestly." What does

the word mean? Liturgical tasks, educational, organizational, functional, managerial? Is he really needed in all of these? In which? Is he hired for the important—but secular—executive-secretary's role in modern society, a heavy hypenation in itself? Could not an unordained Christian do as well? If so, what is the priest to do?[1]

Those eleven Jesuits who contributed their stories as part of *Hyphenated Priests* perhaps feel the day of general practitioners in the priesthood is gone. Or, less categorically, they and others like them maintain that the full-time parish priest has a fine function to fulfill, but that his type of ministry does not exhaust all the possibilities.

No matter. The irrefutable facts are painfully evident. Many priests feel unhappy, confused, restless. For whatever reasons (and they seem to me hopelessly complex and numerous), great numbers have left diocese or community and sought employment elsewhere. The present writer doesn't live in an ivory tower on *this* subject. I just walked into the bedroom and looked at the picture of my class for 1956. Since that ordination date, nine members (nearly 20%) have resigned from the active ministry and labor in a variety of other fields. The majority are married with families of their own, but only a few now work somewhat closely with local parishes in CCD programs or as cantors/lectors/commentators.

In recent years, however, a new dimension has entered the field of clerical departures. Vocal and articulate groups, epitomized probably by the Society of Priests for a Free Ministry, argue for a pluriform priesthood. Previously the clergy who "left" generally did so either reluctantly, with personal sorrow and social stigma, because the burden of celibacy proved too heavy to bear; or determinedly, because they discovered the work of a priest unsatisfying for them or they were unsuited for it. Today a growing number of "former" priests insist the Church needs both married and celibate clergy, part-time and full-time ministers. Former Jesuit Eugene C. Bianchi, president of the free ministry organization, summarizes their position in this excerpt from a May 8, 1970, *National Catholic Reporter* article:

> What are these de-clericalized priests contributing to church reform? They are saying by their actions: "Look, other ways are possible and desirable." They are showing that a priest can be married and self-supporting while deeply involved in pastoral, liturgical and prophetic tasks. The variety of life-styles in SPFM justifies its worth as an experimental project for future ministries.[2]

This demand from some for a freer, more diverse kind of clergy finds support in the works of contemporary writers and continental theologians. Sigur cites Andrew Greeley and his *Religion in the Year 2000* for a projection that "full-time parochial clergy may diminish in relative proportion to part-time specialized or limited-time clergy."[3]

The prolific Chicago priest-sociologist-writer, who claims he has tried to keep in touch with the best of theological studies on the priesthood, particularly by men like Karl Rahner, Edward Schillebeeckx, Hans Küng, and Walter Kasper, also maintains we can no longer define the priest solely in terms of liturgy.

> If there is one position that they universally reject, it is the notion that the priest is primarily a liturgist. Those American clergymen who persist in thinking of the priest as one who leads the liturgy and one who in other respects is no different than anyone else are repeating a theology that is at least five years out of date.[4]

Not everyone buys what Sigur and Greeley and Bianchi seem to be selling. A later issue of *America* contained in response several letters, all negative: one from a parish priest, one from a Jesuit, one from a Redemptorist about to celebrate his silver jubilee of priesthood. Father David E. Delaney from Waltham, Massachusetts, had this to say:

> Having read Msgr. Alexander Sigur's "Today's Priest—GP or More?," let me say that after nine years in the priesthood I get annoyed when I am bombarded with definitions of the priesthood. I like to think that I was aware of what I undertook on the memorable day of ordination. Instead of floundering around for new terms, I think we priests should

be reminded of the great dignity that is ours as diocesan priests. I am all for scholarship and specializing, but I wonder if we are not placing too much stress on the head and neglecting the hearts of our people.[5]

Jubilarian Father Philip J. Lavin, C.SS.R., from Lima, Ohio, finds sad, disappointing, and astonishing the splitting of a priest's identity and the diminution of his role. He cites Pope Paul's message for priests concluding the year of faith in 1968 as more hopeful and encouraging:

To all priests we say: Never doubt the nature of your ministerial priesthood, for it is not a commonplace service for the ecclesial community but one which participates very specially, through orders and an indelible character, in the power of the priesthood of Christ.[6]

The present writer is, I suppose, a hyphenated priest. Even during those dozen years of heavily sacramental work in Syracuse, he served, in the midst of other responsibilities, as athletic director for a small parochial high school. This seems to be as hyphenated as a priest can get. It certainly causes profound identity crises and adequacy anxieties, especially when at basketball, the major sport, your aspiring athletes compile in five years a record of 18 wins and 198 defeats. And now, working in a Washington office, exchanging countless memoranda, he queries, "Is this really a priestly task?" What about the multimedia presentations on love and marriage, the many words churned out by my typewriter? Are these a "priest's" work? More to the point, perhaps, did I in the past or would I in the present find happiness and satisfaction with a restricted, liturgical, sacramental ministry?

Frankly I have clear answers neither to these pointed personal questions nor to those more general, abstract issues surrounding the priesthood in a modern world. I am, like my confreres in the ministry, searching, looking, reaching, very much conscious that we live in a shifting world and a pilgrim Church, very much aware that the kingdom is already, but not yet.

However, I also wonder if we have not been too swift in abandoning the liturgy as a key to the solution of a priest's identity. In the self-evaluation and priesthood-examining process, may we not have unconsciously relegated the ministry at the altar and ambo and font and chair to a side aspect of our lives? I ponder if, in the rush to establish relevancy, we may not have missed or minimized the one area in which we do have competence — leadership in a worship of faith and love.

Soon after my own ordination, Msgr. James P. McPeak, the venerable, ninety-year-old Cathedral rector (he has held the post since 1923), gave his youngest curate some sage advice. "Remain close to those things which produce grace." These words of wisdom may be based on an outdated theology and emanate from the lips of a man naturally not as active as he once was. But since ordination at the turn of our century, he has held every position of power in the diocese, has labored under all the bishops the see has known, and watched hundreds of priests come and go. Experience counts as something, and the counsel of older men as well. We need to include persons like this as resource persons and listen to them, while we at the same moment welcome proposals from others who seek to forge a new world, new horizons, a new priesthood.

Perhaps the past and present, contemporary and classical ways of looking at the ministry are not as disparate as might appear from a surface glance. For example, Greeley relies heavily on the work and writings of Father Walter Kasper, professor of dogmatic theology at the University of Munster. In an essay, "A New Dogmatic Outlook on Priestly Ministry," this scholar attempts to redefine the nature of the priesthood. The following paragraph expresses the key notion of his position.

> In "de-sacralizing" and "de-mythologizing" the priestly office, we not only do justice to the testimony of Scripture, but we also make the priestly office something that is humanly feasible once again. If we reduce the specific nature of this office to the power to pronounce certain words of consecration, then the priestly office is hardly a human vocation that can satisfy the heart of a young man. If, on the other hand, it involves the task of leading the ecclesial

community, then it does indeed involve real human charisms: the ability to meet people and talk with them, the ability to organize and direct human beings, and the capacity for management (in the best sense of that word). Such a task calls for a courteous, responsible and balanced human being, and it demands initiative, imagination and real knowledge of human nature.[7]

Such an explanation merely reinforces what the Council Fathers taught in their Dogmatic Constitution on the Church, Article 28:

By the power of the sacrament of orders, and in the image of Christ the eternal High Priest (Heb. 5:1-10: 7:24; 9:11-28), they are consecrated to preach the gospel, shepherd the faithful, and celebrate divine worship as true priests of the New Testament. . . . They exercise this sacred function of Christ most of all in the Eucharistic liturgy or synaxis. There, acting in the person of Christ, and proclaiming His mystery, they join the offering of the faithful to the sacrifice of their Head.[8]

The present volume on a celebrant's role revolves around this Vatican II teaching that the ultimate functions of a priest are to shepherd the faithful, preach the gospel, and celebrate divine worship. We may quibble about the extension of these root tasks to specific areas, but agreement on them as essential features of what the priest is and does, establishes a tone or attitude and fixes values or priorities. With those established and fixed in mind and heart, the priest should find they exert an extremely pragmatic impact on his approach to the liturgy.

1. *Shepherd the faithful.* Standing in front of the church before Sunday services is, as we mentioned, a wearing task, but not an unpleasant one. And its pastoral value cannot be debated. People come to Mass, some happy, others sad; some cheerful and outgoing, others gloomy and withdrawn; some open and friendly, others distant, even hostile. Most arrive preoccupied with their own personal worries or anticipating an event later in the day.

Our lives, however, hopefully center around the parish, the Eucharist, the persons in our care. Very few parishioners, on the contrary, organize their lives around us. For the majority we form only a part of their world, a portion more or less important, more or less a duty, more or less inspirational.

The priest who faithfully stands in front of the church week after week displays a concern for his flock, gets to know his people a bit better, and silently indicates his interested availability. He may also by a simple smile or cheerful word unknowingly lift a despondent soul out of the doldrums or bring a self-centered individual out of his shell. He is, in a word, building community, making contact, and elevating people out of their isolated selves and into congregational worship.

It seems we have now reached a level in which, at least for the major Sunday services, we should plan to have the celebrant vest in the narthex, enter and leave by procession through the central aisle, and remain at the door to shake hands after Mass. This gesture alone can do much to transform for people a dull, impersonal, routine weekly obligation into a pleasant, personal, refreshing Sabbath celebration.

2. *Preach the gospel.* Preaching the word may be interpreted to include countless efforts quite distantly removed from the celebration of the liturgy strictly defined. It is not our purpose here to debate the rightness or wrongness of that view. We instead merely plead for well-prepared, contemporary, succinct homilies; (multimedia man's attention span for sermons is, I think, no more than ten minutes). That is to say, if a priest accepts the definition given and considers gospel-preaching as one of his primary functions, we trust he will apportion time and effort accordingly.

During a well-attended lecture for the laity on liturgical change in Joliet, Illinois, just before the introduction of the revised Order of Mass, a participant asked the speaker what was being done to improve the quality of Sunday sermons. He replied with a question, "Do you think they need improvement?" The spontaneous and sustained applause which immediately followed gave him the answer.

At suburban Blessed Sacrament Parish in Alexandria, Virginia, across the Potomac from Washington, the recently organized parish liturgical committee helps plan the theme, hymns, commentaries and homilies for every Sunday. This supplies the priests with ongoing input for their message, aids them in understanding what are the concerns of parishioners, and gives each one honest and constructive criticisms with which to evaluate his performance.

The procedure in Alexandria works much better when one priest preaches at all the Masses on a given Sunday. Granted the ideal of a celebrant delivering his own homily, I wonder if today in large parishes this is the most effective procedure. Will, in fact, a priest work that hard at preparation week after week? Can one man weekly develop a moving presentation filled with examples, practical applications, and spiritual insights into current events? How do several priests in one parish, preaching each week at different Masses, coordinate their labors especially on sensitive issues like race, war and peace, abortion? Isn't it a waste for a few people only to hear a particularly superb sermon when all could benefit? Won't the preacher who delivers the same homily four or five times ultimately polish and perfect it through the repetition? Will he not learn through the day what "touches" the congregation and what doesn't, how to cut here and expand there? Doesn't an every two, three, or four week preaching schedule, with an announcement of speaker and topic in the bulletin, put indirect pressure on the priest to work harder at his preaching?

Obviously in smaller parishes this type of method is impossible. But even there, an occasional weekend exchange of pulpit (and confessional) might present a fresh face and different approach for people accustomed to the same man week after week.

The key, however, is attitude. If a priest believes in God's word and possesses a strong commitment to preaching the gospel, he will take pains, whatever the practical steps followed, to prepare conscientiously for those precious few moments in which he speaks with his people.

3. *Celebrate divine worship.* If one concurs with Kasper and Küng about the centrality of eucharistic celebrations in the life of the Church and of the priest, then those moments when Christians gather around the altar become most important. Sunday services in that context cease being a chore, an in-and-out of the parking lot, a get-the-collection-counted experience, and take on the character of a happy, satisfying, even if enervating, event. Activities during the week considered in this light should point to and flow from these hours when parishioners assemble to break bread and celebrate Christ's Resurrection. Because the Eucharist does occupy, in my judgment, the central and pivotal place in the life of a priest and a parish, we need to examine this truth in greater detail.

Chapter 6

LEADER OF CHRISTIAN WORSHIP

On Mother's Day in 1970, student protest against the foray of United States armed forces into Cambodia was at fever pitch. In a suburban parish on that spring Sunday, a young deacon, deeply troubled by the domestic developments, preached in rather strong terms about war and peace, freedom and fascism. Not all in the pews were pleased. About two dozen stormed out, slamming doors as they did so. A few more vocal opponents loudly objected to his homily, told him to step down from the pulpit, and let the celebrant go on with Mass. After the distribution of Communion and before the dismissal, he apologized for the temper of his remarks and indicated a regret they had caused such pain and offended so many. The congregation broke out into spontaneous applause.

It was an interesting Sabbath celebration, to say the least. One wife and mother, hoping to hear on this day a few words in church about Mary or motherhood, quivered with rage and wept in indignation at this "Communist" turning God's house into a political forum. Two other ladies, visibly disturbed by the rudeness of these critics and the crudity of their remarks, were shocked at this unheard-of demonstration in church. A few individuals stopped and congratulated or consoled the shaken deacon. Apparently the undercurrent of hatred, unrest, and polarization in the parish, community, and nation had erupted, triggered by this well-intentioned preacher of peace.

What about his course of action? Wise or imprudent? Honest or insensitive? Courageous or impetuous? Faithful to the prophetic role of a priest or careless in his function as a conciliator? Was he proclaiming the gospel of Jesus, probing consciences, raising gut issues? Or was he dividing the community, becoming too specific, aligning himself with concrete, detailed, and therefore debatable solutions? Difficult questions indeed, ones which I am sure only God can answer. The parishioners obviously shared divergent views on his presentation and even the young man himself must wonder, "Was I right, was I wrong?"

What, then, is a priest? The prophet who speaks in Jeremiah-like fashion to his people or the conciliator who heals wounds with a Franciscan message of love? As a prophet, one who fearlessly preaches God's Word, he often will walk alone, will frequently run ahead of his flock, will not hesitate to condemn existing institutions—ecclesiastical or civil—which seem to have forgotten the gospel in the pressure of preserving a bureaucracy. As a reconciler, one who continuously seeks unity among men, he will be standing in the middle, will sometimes be accused of game-playing and dishonesty, will occasionally encounter hatred and misunderstanding from both sides.

Leon-Joseph Cardinal Suenens seems like a good person to ask about these matters. He has stood alone, has spoken out, has used both political cunning and personal courage to change Church structures. But at the same time, Suenens undoubtedly pictures himself as a peacemaker, as a bishop attempting to bind his people together in the Spirit, as a priest seeking to end polarization and bitterness among men. His book, *Co-Responsibility in the Church*, reflects that latter notion and contains what this writer thinks is perhaps the finest contemporary description of a bishop's role.

The bishop of today, having recognized and situated this tension, must be, more than ever before, the living link between the generations. Even at the risk of seeming too progressive to the older generations or too fearful in the judgment of the young, he must join within himself the past and the future, the tradition to be safeguarded and the progress to be made. This means that we must have a living and serene faith in the Holy Spirit at work in the Church yesterday, today and tomorrow.[1]

I suppose in reality bishop or priest must be both prophet and conciliator, depending on the situation, the times, the circumstances. However, in either case it would appear that he exercises his function primarily when serving as the designated leader of worship. This is when the People of God assemble, this is when the Church becomes, this is the occasion for a prophetic word of rebuke or a conciliatory message of healing. That is the time for such things, if we accept Küng's concept of the Church expressed in the following excerpt:

But Christ is above all present and active in the worship of the congregation. . . . Here God speaks to the Church through his word, and the Church speaks to God by replying in its prayers and its song of praise. Here the crucified and risen Lord becomes present through his word and sacrament, and here we commit ourselves to his service: by hearing his Gospel in faith, by confessing our sins, by praising God's mercy and by petitioning the Father in Jesus' name, by taking part in the meal of the Lord who is present among us and by providing the basis for our service of one another by our public confession of faith and by praying for one another. This is fundamentally where the Church is, where the Church, the community, the congregation happens.[2]

The Council Fathers at Vatican II maintained a similar position in their document on the liturgy.

> The bishop is to be considered the high priest of his flock.
> In a certain sense it is from him that the faithful who are
> under his care derive and maintain their life in Christ.
>
> Therefore all should hold in very high esteem the li-
> turgical life of the diocese which centers around the bishop,
> especially in his cathedral church. Let them be persuaded
> that the Church reveals herself most clearly when a full
> complement of God's holy people, united in prayer and in a
> common liturgical service (especially the Eucharist), exer-
> cise a thorough and active participation at the very altar
> where the bishop presides in the company of his priests and
> other assistants.[3]

To be quite honest, some priests find this description of the
bishop and of his relationship to the people in a diocese dreamy
and "hard-to-swallow." They have had their hands slapped for
alleged "experimentation" with the liturgy; they seldom see
bishops and know that, for the majority of the laity, he is only a
name or a photograph on the rectory wall; they have received in
the past worship directives from chancery offices which stressed
minute rules, but ignored the underlying spirit; they used to
attend the solemn cathedral functions, but now tend to avoid
them because of their impersonalism, lack of warmth, and clerical tone. (One sadly recalls a bishop's ordination recently in
which the sign of peace was passed twice around the sanctuary,
at the ordination itself and before Communion, but never
reached beyond the sanctuary to priests, religious, and laity in
the pews). They judge, finally, that in many ways the bishop
himself is a "poor celebrant" and cannot bring themselves to
regard him as the model liturgist for their diocese.

These reactions surely are understandable. The priest dedicated to providing warm, meaningful worship for his parishioners and deeply hurt or badly disillusioned by anonymous criticisms from above, by specific rebukes from his bishop, and by
restrictive legislation from the liturgical commission cannot easily wax enthusiastic about the theology of this Article 41 in the
Liturgy Constitution. They cannot forget the human, imperfect

embodiment of that ideal in a man and in the men who have caused them such pain in earlier days.

To those men wounded in battle, justly or unjustly, in reality or in their imagination, I would not dare to speak glibly or with condescension. One does not talk in trite cliches about the cross to those who once suffered on the tree or now carry it upon their backs. I only address to them a word of history and a note of hope.

This bishop-surrounded-by-his-people concept of the Church and its liturgy is not a fresh notion concocted by 2,000 men in Rome trying to confirm their positions of authority. It is an ancient, early Christian approach of individuals like St. Ignatius of Antioch, persons who similarly shared the Master's martyrdom and experienced in their own bodies his passion. Jungmann's *The Mass of the Roman Rite* indicates that nearly all accounts of the liturgy we have from the end of the first until well into the fourth century presume the primitive and original arrangement of Mass celebration in which the bishop surrounded by his clergy offers up the sacrifice in the presence of a congregation. The Austrian scholar likewise points out that this perdured as a model for celebration much longer both in the West and in the East. "Thus the ideal form for uniting the whole community of the episcopal see in one service and promoting the complete self-oblation of the community remained alive for long in the consciousness of the occidental Church. In the Orient this is still the case today."[4]

Naturally, the world today is bigger, more complex; patterns of worship suitable in small Christian assemblies centuries ago may not prove satisfactory for contemporary society. But, "the times they are achanging" and these trends do spell out hope for celebrants and laity vitally concerned about the Church and its worship. We know that greater delegation by ordinaries of diocesan business (e. g., clerical appointments to personnel boards, worship concerns to liturgical commissions) leaves added freedom for episcopal, "pastoral" visitation. Further, we read reports about an increasing number of bishops who rotate on Sundays around parishes to offer Mass, preach a homily, and meet with parishioners after the service. In addition, the willingness to permit home Masses, to establish floating, interest-oriented communities, to send men for advanced liturgical studies suggests a commitment to quality worship on the local level. Finally, the publication of more officially flexible rites from Rome and the possibility of legitimate adaptation to particular situations reduces somewhat the gap between what the Church allows and what the concerned liturgist deems necessary.

This writer has experienced at clergy conferences in Pittsfield, Massachusetts, and Bolton, Connecticut, living demonstrations of the liturgy's power to unite bishop and presbyterate around the altar. After a day-long series of lectures on the revised Order of Mass and the rites for baptism and marriage, the several hundred assembled at each place joined in a carefully planned, fully participated Eucharist. One bishop sat with the main body of priests in the pews, the other joined as a simple concelebrant. Both dispensed from general Church legislation and allowed the clerics to communicate, even if they had already offered or were to celebrate a parish Mass later. There was real force in those Masses, a feeling of coming together, the sense of brotherhood and involvement in a common cause. Bishop Christopher Weldon of Springfield remarked a month afterwards that this joint offering of the "new" Mass did much to soften the acrimony, the polarization which had developed throughout his diocese in past years between old and young priests, between progressive and conservative clergy.

Marvelous as such conferences may be, the fact remains that a bishop, regardless of how imaginative and missionary, cannot always and everywhere care personally for the spiritual needs of his people. Article 42 of the Constitution on the Liturgy recognizes this and sees the parish priest in effect as a "little bishop."

> But because it is impossible for the bishop always and everywhere to preside over the whole flock in his Church, he cannot do other than establish lesser groupings of the faithful. Among these, parishes set up locally under a pastor who takes the place of the bishop are the most important:

for in a certain way they represent the visible Church as it is established throughout the world.[5]

There are some practical consequences which flow from this principle. First of all, it seems to me that a cathedral requires only one presidential chair. When the rector or an associate offers Mass he, like any celebrant, does so precisely in the name of and as a representative for the bishop. Other ways can be employed, if deemed necessary, to demonstrate that the bishop, not his delegate, is the leader of worship for a given occasion.

Secondly, since the liturgical celebrant extends, as it were, the hand, voice, and person of a bishop, he consequently needs to be united in mind and heart with that shepherd who leads his diocese. The teaching of early Christian Fathers cited earlier certainly would support this assertion. We simply must deplore, in the light of this norm, a situation in which the bishop and his priest are at odds: where there is not harmony: where, for instance, the actions of a celebrant and the directives of his ordinary openly clash. Fortunately, due to a variety of reasons, these personal misunderstandings and public conflicts have diminished greatly in the period following introduction of the revised liturgical books.

Thirdly, while it may bolster the ego of a priest to regard himself as a "little bishop," he should understand that responsibilities which accompany this title are by no means minimal. The celebrant, like the bishop, therefore, ought to serve as both prophet and conciliator in the manner sketched by Cardinal Suenens. He needs to unite his people and heal the wounds of divisiveness. Any pastor, any parish priest knows how difficult, lonely, and frustrating that task sometimes can be.

Vatican II had some further words to offer about the bishop, the parish, and especially the Sunday celebration.

> Therefore the liturgical life of the parish and its relationship to the bishop must be fostered in the thinking and practice of both laity and clergy; efforts also must be made to encourage a sense of community within the parish, above all in the common celebration of the Sunday Mass.[6]

If the Church fundamentally happens, occurs, becomes, when Christians unite for the Eucharist, we can also maintain that this particularly holds true when those Eucharistic services celebrate the Resurrection on Easter and on the fifty-one other "little Easters" throughout the year. Each Sunday enjoys a special prerogative in the restored Church calendar. Moreover, the central thrust of liturgical reform certainly is its insistence upon the primacy of Christ's paschal mystery. All of the revised texts revolve around this theme and attempt to express it in clear, simple rites which need little or no explanation.

As I have observed in another place, the priest who accepts these theological points as bases for his ministry regards Sundays in a different light. They are the high points of each week for him, and every Sunday becomes the happy, well-prepared, anticipated occasion when his people meet with their leader for worship.

We have problems here, as all engaged in pastoral work know well. Frequent and lengthy letters from the bishop read at the pulpit neither bind people to their ordinary nor move them to the desired action. They generally bore parishioners to death or send them daydreaming about the afternoon's golf game. Bishops must discover new and more potent methods of communicating to the flock. So, too, large parishes and huge churches present almost insuperable obstacles to "a sense of community within the parish." I, for one, do not plead for the end of territorial parishes. Like the poor, I feel they will always be with us and that the liturgical renewal will probably rise or fall to the extent that we revitalize parish worship. At the same time, however, creation of imaginative, optional communities, division of mammoth plants, and construction of smaller, inexpensive churches might help ease the impersonalism we presently face in many areas.

Still, and this is the essential reason for the present volume, the priest, the celebrant, the pastor carries the brunt of that burden. He can without doubt ruin worship and bring near despair to his people if he doesn't care, doesn't believe, doesn't understand. On the other hand, if he does care and believe and understand, he may be able to move his flock. But not necessarily.

The roadblocks to good worship today, hinted at above, are immense and numerous. But if the celebrant has faith in Christ's presence, believes in the priesthood, and is committed to divine worship, he may just find his Catholic people are becoming, Sunday after Sunday, more Christian through this weekly celebration of Jesus' paschal mystery.

Chapter 7

A HEALTHY REGARD
FOR RUBRICS

The story is told of a young, freshly ordained Brooklyn priest, summoned out of his rectory in the wee hours of the morning to care for a terminally ill patient in one of the local hospitals. After hanging up the receiver, this eager, serious, dedicated man of God dressed quickly, opened up the church, placed a host in his pyx, and drove to the hospital.

Following the traditional confession, prayers, and anointing, he prepared to give his patient Viaticum. However, nervous and awkward because of inexperience, the youthful cleric accidentally dropped the host. Somewhat panic-stricken at first, he quickly regained his composure, picked up the Blessed Sacrament, and placed it on the person's tongue.

In a few moments he began to fret about particles which might have remained on the spot where it had fallen. Considerable prayer and painful reflection over the matter led him to summon a nurse and ask her to change the bed. She thought this was a bit odd, but wishing to avoid difficulty with the night supervisor, she removed the sheet and handed it over to him. The assistant carefully folded the white linen, tucked it under his arm, and returned by car to the rectory.

He reopened the church and walked to the sacristy, fully intending to wash his tightly held and precious burden in the sacrarium. But the late hour, yesterday's full day and tomorrow's fuller one, prompted him to take a different course of action. Instead he unlocked the tabernacle, stuffed the linen into this compartment, and went quickly to his room hoping to rescue a few moments of sleep from the abbreviated night. He expected, of course, to rise early, before the first parish Mass, and purify the bed sheet now safely stored over the altar.

But, alas, the weary priest overslept. His pastor, offering the 7:00 A.M. Eucharist and unaware of the curate's traumatic experience, suspected nothing out of the ordinary until Communion time. Then, as he opened the tabernacle door, the good monsignor noticed a corner of cloth protruding between the decorative curtains and started pulling and pulling and pulling.

The pastor and his assistant dialogued that morning at breakfast.

This tale, fundamentally true, although slightly embellished through clerical retelling, illustrates the kind of rubrical fetishism which all too often has kept and even continues to keep celebrants from a relaxed and natural comfortableness during the liturgy. It is the contention of this chapter that priests should possess a healthy respect and regard for the rubrics, but not make idols of them. They are significantly serious norms, principles, and guidelines for good worship; but they are neither divinely inspired nor objects of value in themselves, only important means to a noble end.

In the course of my years in pastoral work I have acquired four personal rules or rubrics to govern liturgical celebrations.

1. *Lex suprema, salus animarum.* This motto of Bishop McQuaid, founder of St. Bernard's Seminary in Rochester (where precise rubrics indeed were followed, as its older alumni will readily testify), stands as *the* rubric, *the* one inviolable principle, *the* sole unbreakable regulation. To serve people and save them is the priest's task and the liturgy's function. In doing so he and it will glorify God and praise the Lord.

2. *Do the best you can.* Remarkable Msgr. McPeak, the Cathedral rector cited earlier, learned this bit of pastoral wisdom from a seminary professor and has passed it on to the many priests who have served under his tutelage. Hardly world shaking in its originality and simply rooted in common sense, the adage nevertheless tends to keep an overregulated modern man and contemporary priest from losing perspective.

3. *Sacramenta sunt propter homines.* We studied moral theology in seminary from Noldin-Schmitt's *Summa Theologiae Moralis* under the guidance of a very thorough, disciplined, and, I must say, devout priest-instructor. There were in those days the infinite number of distinctions and divisions, including a brief section in which we analyzed *"Quantum peccatum sit sacramentum administrare in statu peccati."* Hidden in the text, however, the reader could discover, *"Cum enim sacramenta instituta sint propter homines, administrari possunt in statu peccati, potius quam salus animae periclitetur."*[1] This notion that Christ instituted the sacraments for men, for people was not denied, of course, but somehow it never permeated the whole approach to moral or pastoral theology.

It became a real and operative principle for me when I observed a holy, octogenarian priest follow it day after day in his ministry. Msgr. Angelo Strazzoni served during those times as chaplain at St. Mary's Hospital in Syracuse, heard confessions each Saturday at the Cathedral, and was the diocesan clergy's most popular confessor. In my early years I probably thought of him as a laxist; but later, and wiser, I realized he really possessed the mind of Jesus with regard to his priesthood. Pardon, mercy, goodness, love, service, comfort, help—the sacraments, according to Father Angelo, should bring these things to people.

4. *Liturgy is for men, not men for the liturgy.* Pope Paul VI, then Cardinal Montini, said it. I don't have the text before me, but believe he spoke these words during discussions about the Liturgy Constitution at the Council's first session. No matter. Regardless of who uttered the words or when, this message rings true.

We should strive for excellence in our worship programs, but not because liturgy is a goal within itself. Liturgical celebrations are for God and for men. Good liturgy enables people to pray better, to praise the Lord more effectively, to drink richer shares of divine life through the sacred rites. It accomplishes those goals through contact with human persons and to the extent that individuals are moved internally by a ceremony or service.

These four root principles support the assertion that we should not idolize the rubrics nor ever make a fetish of them. We quoted in our introduction the Roman Missal's General Instruction, Article 6, along this vein. "This instruction is intended to give general guidelines for celebrating the eucharist and also norms for each form of the celebration."[2] These are norms and guidelines, not God-given, unchangeable, irreplaceable commands. They have been designed solely to "foster active and full participation and promote the spiritual welfare of the faithful."[3]

There is, however, another side of the coin, a balancing part of the equation. Celebrants also need to possess a healthy regard for the rubrics. The reformed liturgical texts cannot be classified as a "do your own thing," "build it yourself," Erector Set kit of documents. More general, yes; multiple options, yes; richer selections, yes; greater freedom, yes. Total liberty, no; unrestricted choices, no; devoid of directions, no. The revised liturgical books contain rites carefully selected, carefully researched, pastorally tested. They include extensive variations from which the priest may choose, and they give to national conferences of bishops the right, even the duty, to make additional adaptations when the authorized ceremony and texts prove inadequate or unsatisfactory. But those new publications presume celebrants will honor the norms with due consideration, attempt to understand these reforms, and follow them in practice whenever possible. It makes good sense.

First of all, the Eucharist involves tradition, a sacred one at that. "Do this in memory of me." The celebrant, "little bishop" that he is, must function as a living link with the cherished past. To manifest a sensible respect for the rubrics indicates concern for our Christian heritage, awareness of an ongoing, continuous chain of events in salvation history. The Council Fathers spoke of this when they posited certain norms for the liturgical reforms.

> That sound tradition may be retained, and yet the way be open for legitimate progress, a careful investigation is always to be made into each part of the liturgy which is to be revised. This investigation should be theological, historical, and pastoral. Also, the general laws concerning the structure and meaning of the liturgy must be studied in conjunction with the experience derived from recent liturgical reforms and from the indults conceded to various places. Finally, there must be no innovations unless the good of the Church genuinely and certainly requires them; and care must be taken that any new forms adopted should in some way grow organically from forms already existing.[4]

Secondly, we as priests do seem to show a tendency toward eccentricities. Pretty much prima donnas, at least in the past (perhaps less so in the "new" Church), we need some kind of regulations to keep our odd habits within limits and spare a congregation complete consternation. Granted that the recent norms are more flexible and permit a greater expression of individuality — praiseworthy progress — the faithful at the same time do enjoy a corresponding right to recognize that it is a Mass which we are offering! Healthy regard for the rubrics without getting "uptight" about them can preserve a basic unity in the midst of accidental diversity. Pope Paul VI mentioned this unity-diversity concept in his Apostolic Constitution promulgating the restored Roman Missal.

> There is room in the new Missal, according to the decree of the Second Vatican Council, "for legitimate variations and adaptations," but we hope that it will be received by the faithful as a help and witness to the common unity of all. Thus, in the great diversity of languages, one single prayer will rise as an acceptable offering to our Father in heaven, through our High Priest, Jesus Christ, in the Holy Spirit.[5]

Finally, the celebrant who stands in the pulpit hopefully speaks as his master did, with authority. In today's world, the power, the establishment, and the decisions from above are constantly questioned. But even more, the sincerity and honesty of a man with responsibility or authority are subject to severe scrutiny. A priest who seeks to preach the gospel message with force, who asks his people to follow him in the hard issues of race, war, peace, and brotherhood, is actually asking them to accept his spiritual authority. If they know he lightly regards the Church's regulations in different areas, including worship, I fear they will consider only casually his directives on Christian living.

A healthy respect for the rubrics should create a climate in which the celebrant can be relaxed, but reverent, natural, but dignified. We will now develop these points.

Chapter 8

RELAXED AND NATURAL

We have commented in earlier chapters on the precise rubrics which have governed liturgical celebrations since publication of the missal by Pius V. Establishment of the Sacred Congregation of Rites a few years later further insured that worship in the Roman Catholic Church would be carefully watched over and regulated by curial officials at the Holy See. These developments corrected then current abuses and protected the liturgy for four centuries from harmful influences.

However, in the recent past it became clear that what once was a blessing—the rigid, frozen Roman rite—now had taken on the character of a burden. Inflexible and unadaptable to local conditions, the traditional liturgical texts and rubrics seemed divorced from real life. Moreover, the many commentaries, interpretations, and official decrees appended to Pius V's original missal placed the celebrant in something of a straitjacket. He had little opportunity to stamp a service with his own personality. In fact, the priest who dared to do so was considered to be infected with stubborn pride, unwilling to suppress his individualism and conform to the Church's regulations.

Paul VI's revised Roman Missal follows a different path. By supplying general guidelines and liberal rubrics it leaves much to the judgment of each celebrant. It presumes that a priest, usually ordained in his middle twenties, is mature enough to decide how his hands should be extended, how a bow should be made, how he should kiss the altar. It implies, I think, that if he does not possess such sufficient good sense and cannot celebrate well according to these free regulations, he must not be ordained nor allowed to preside any longer at public worship.

More positively, the General Instruction and Order of Mass frees the cleric for a relaxed, natural, pleasant style of leadership at prayer and permits the addition of his own distinctive temperament to the universal gospel of Jesus. While we strongly maintain Christ baptizes, anoints, presides, we also hold that the Lord acts in these sacraments through a unique, individual, human person. The infinite mystery of God's presence and divine grace in sacred signs is in no way diminished by emphasis on the distinctness of the flesh and blood instrument involved.

Pastoral experience confirms that no priest can reach everyone. His personality attracts some, repels others. His manner of celebration impresses a few and leaves many unmoved. His way of working will bring some back to God who have resisted the efforts of predecessors, but fail to touch others however hard he labors. The boundless depth of our Creator and the unlimited variety of his creatures call for an equivalent diversity of priests who can serve these people. The new rubrics fortunately rest on that principle.

In many ways these reforms come at a providential moment in salvation history. The wave of today's personalism has affected clergy and laity alike. Couples seek a wedding ceremony peculiarly their own, not a stereotyped reproduction of what others have done. Penitents abhor routine confessions and avoid the sacrament entirely unless they find some way or some one to make the encounter personal for them. So, too, young men must sense a certain individual fulfillment in the ministry, feel they contribute in a special way to the priesthood, or their spirits become restless and they turn away, looking for a different challenge, an alternate channel for these creative talents. Perhaps the revised liturgy will help stem these trends and provide a type of worship services and work styles suitable for modern man.

But what do we mean by a natural and relaxed style of leadership? This needs to be spelled out more specifically, in greater detail, and with practical applications. In amplifying these concepts, I am indebted to the Milwaukee Archdiocesan Liturgical Commission for some of their suggestions on the role of the celebrant in the flexible liturgy. I also am grateful to Father Robert Hovda, whose article a few years back pioneered most of the discussion on style and presence in celebration.[1]

The priest who celebrates this revised liturgy should be:

1. *Himself.* The celebrant, it is true, must in many ways serve as a performer, but he likewise needs to avoid artificial acting. Projecting cheerfulness and tranquillity to a Sunday congregation when one is inwardly depressed or anxious is one thing; behaving out of character is quite another. For one celebrant a smile comes as his most natural response to the presence of people before him in the pews. For other priests, however, smiling at the congregation during the Eucharist would be unnatural, forced, phoney.

Hovda says this well:

> Many men undergo a kind of transformation, a total change of voice, tone, inflection, the minute they smell sanctuary dust. This "pulpit tone" must be laid to rest at once, for the sake of the honest, authentic style and presence our times, even more than times past, now demand. Any suggestion of fakery or falsity or the assuming of a "sacred alias" must be consciously avoided. We can't even trust our own judgment in this matter, because the habit is a subtle one. We have to ask a friend so close that he can criticize: "Do I sound like myself—certainly at my noblest and best, but *like myself*?"[2]

2. *Relaxed.* The relaxed celebrant by his very being creates an atmosphere of peace and easiness. At Bishop Edwin Broderick's marvelous installation ceremony in Albany, New York, the new ordinary communicated these qualities by simple ges-

tures. He smiled, shook hands, spoke with each of the eighteen gift-bearing persons in the offertory procession. He greeted, saluted, embraced at the sign of peace bishops, priests, ministers, rabbis, relatives, and friends. He preached a homily in frank terms about his human limitations. People relax when they are happy and feel happy when relaxed. They also pray better when the surrounding climate is easy, comfortable, joyous. Guests sensed these things on that day in Albany and prayed well, mainly because of the way in which their new bishop functioned as a celebrant.

Milwaukee's Commission links this relaxed image with a human approach.

> The celebrant must present a relaxed image to the congregation if he is to express its unity. Since the letter kills and the spirit gives life, any excessive concern with rubrics will show itself in an artificiality of presence and a certain un-human feeling in his activity. Ritualism can smack of magic. The celebrant is human, therefore flexible. He can communicate this human spirit in his comments made during celebration. . . . This type of comment is not an addition to the liturgy, but an accepted part of his office as teacher. Whereas the celebrant's constant interruption is distracting, smooth explanation can facilitate intelligent participation, e.g., explaining the kiss of peace as sign of unity and forgiveness.[3]

3. *Reverent and gracious.* Being relaxed and natural should not be confused with or become an excuse for casualness and disrespect. Holy things ought to be treated in a holy way. Any priest with deeply grounded faith in the multipresence of Christ summarized by Article 7 of the Liturgy Constitution will have few difficulties in this regard. That type of celebrant knows these are sublime, sacred moments calling for reverence and respect, care and concern. Similarly, his understanding of God's Holy People and recognition of an individual person's supreme dignity should help him avoid manipulation of others and insensitivity to their feelings. Leadership by shock may be in vogue for the moment on the political scene. The model liturgical leader, however, on the contrary is a gentle man, truly man, truly gentle, who raises hopes and hearts, not eyebrows and hatreds.

The preceding remarks should make it clear that reverence cannot be identified with folded hands, downcast eyes, pained expressions. Neither is casual sauntering around the sanctuary an essential sign of a relaxed and natural celebrant. These qualities basically exist in the heart and are only manifested through the body. The trick is to have one's external being reflect the noblest throughts of his interior self and to steer a middle course between excessive familiarity and artificial formalism.

4. *Confident*. The priest who enjoys natural self-confidence probably finds liturgical services a relatively easy part of his daily duties. The less gifted person must work harder at them. Nevertheless, both richly endowed celebrants and more diffident individuals need to understand what the liturgy is all about and to prepare carefully for each service if they are to conduct themselves in the confident way we are talking about at this point.

The leadership role entails bringing together a number of people who have different functions to perform. Unless a celebrant clearly grasps the role of each, and directs them accordingly, the total liturgy suffers. A priest, for example, who allows ushers to start the collection during the general intercessions has failed to give proper guidance, creates confusion among the people, upsets both ushers and commentators, and ends up flustered himself.

Similarly, the celebrant who has not carefully marked the books beforehand or who has not prepared his prayers, readings, and homily in advance will flounder around, waste precious minutes looking for the proper page and, in general, give parishioners a feeling of uncertainty. Even the cockiest priest can no longer fool his people if he does not allocate some time for planning the liturgy. There are simply too many options. Confidence means being on top of a situation. In worship these days, that requires above all adequate knowledge and preparatory effort.

The priest who doesn't feel terribly sure of himself should not despair. A willingness to study liturgy and work at worship are far more important than natural self-confidence. Moreover, faith in the fact that Christ acts through his celebrant ought to reassure the hesitant priest that if he conscientiously does his best, the grace of God will do the rest.

5. *Dignified.* Father Hovda feels that the physical bearing of the celebrant can communicate a sense of his dignity and purpose; he applies this in an eminently practical way to the manner in which the priest vests for a liturgical celebration.

> These new days call for a certain bearing, just as the old days did. In the old days, for one reason or another, the bearing of the leader of our worship frequently suggested the carrying of a very heavy weight. . . .
>
> But these are new days. The president represents the whole body of Christ, the whole community. His posture, his walk, his bearing must speak of humble power and dignity and purpose. He is not a traffic cop, always ready for assault. He is not a bureaucrat, fatigued by the long queue in front of his office. He is not a worm, defeated by the pain and suffering of life. He is a free man chosen to be Christ's man, and this is what his carriage must convey.
>
> As long as we use vesture for the ministers of our public worship, they must manifest the dignity of the person and of the occasion by carefully dressing up. The embarrassment mentioned above is never more evident than in the clownish, haphazard manner in which many celebrants fling on the vestments. Dressing up, in church or elsewhere, is an expression of one's love and one's respect for others. A ministry that disdains this lacks charity as much as it lacks sophistication.[4]

6. *Warm and friendly.* The extrovert who loves people, who enjoys being with them and grows moody or restless when alone too long, is warm and friendly by nature. The shy, introspective, quiet priest, on the other hand, must push himself to greet the people at Mass, meet a sudden rush of strangers at wedding rehearsals, or mix easily with the noisy and distracted crowd at Sunday afternoon baptisms.

Despite the present declericalization of the Church and a shift in the attitude of some toward the clergy, I feel the priest continues for many to stand as a sign and symbol of God, Christ, the Church. Rightly or wrongly, the experience of these people with an individual cleric dictates much of their subsequent feelings about religion in general and Catholicism in particular. This spirit of warmth and friendliness, then, not only creates a receptive climate for community worship; it also forms positive impressions which will carry over for future years.

The priest needs to exercise caution lest his friendly attention be directed to a few favorites rather than to all the parishioners. It takes little effort to speak with the young, the attractive, the intelligent, the important, the personable. It takes great love to converse with the old, the homely, the simple, the abandoned, the eccentric. If a celebrant caters to his less noble self in this regard, then warmth and friendliness, praiseworthy in itself, becomes instead divisive and hurtful.

7. *Enthusiastic and happy.* Not every priest is constitutionally warm and friendly, nor is every cleric naturally enthusiastic and happy. We shouldn't force ourselves to act artificially here either. False enthusiasm and a contrived "bubbling over" make people wince; they prefer in that case a serene, but honest seriousness.

However, especially in this modern era weighted down with more than its share of despair, cynicism, and misery, a celebrant's joy and enthusiasm can prove infectious. They assert that life is worth living, that men can change the world and resolve its problems, that the comforts of life exceed by far its crosses. They quietly teach something to others about this man's personal faith and hope. They really reflect his inner happiness over the fact that he and these people have gathered to celebrate, to praise God for the marvelous mystery of life, both human and divine.

8. *Humble.* An awareness of his position as an instrument of the Lord Jesus can give strength and courage to a celebrant; at the same time it should make him exceedingly humble. The liturgy is really God's work, not ours, and the worshiping community his People, not ours. The priest plays an important, significant role—the pages of this book reiterate that point. Yet the marvels of grace and the wonders Christ's Spirit works in men never cease. We preach a supposedly superb homily and discover it apparently touched no one. We drag ourselves away from the pulpit convinced that the day's message fell on deaf ears, only to reap a rich harvest in the confessional several weeks

later. Frequent lessons like these can keep the prayerful cleric profoundly humble.

The celebrant needs a certain human-oriented humility as well. No longer, obviously, does a priest possess all the answers. There are bright, well-educated, serious-minded people in that church. They are busy and preoccupied and critical. These individuals want services to start on time, sermons to be well-prepared, and ceremonies to be carried out with meaning. They cannot and will not squander precious moments on mediocre performances. Oh, they will, many of them, out of loyalty and through a deeply ingrained sense of obligation, but in frank discussion one hears justified objections and catches the deep resentment.

The priest, conscious of his serious obligations before God and his heavy responsibility toward men, won't require a monthly day of recollection to maintain proper humility.

9. *Strong.* Should the celebrant reflect his ups and downs, his joys and sorrows to the community before him? More to the point, is it wise for a priest at the altar or in the pulpit to reveal his inner doubts and anxieties, his intimate failures and uncertainties? These are interesting and, unfortunately, quite relevant questions. Few clerics today, I fear, feel totally free of personal or vocational turbulence.

Some would argue that contemporary man admires openness, sincerity, frankness and thus a priest who puts human frailty on public display cannot help but win over his congregation. Others maintain that mankind must always have its idols, its heroes, its leaders, and that troubled parishioners with ample burdens and hesitations of their own look to the shepherd for guidance, strength, sureness.

Those who hold this second opinion urge celebrants to push aside, as it were, some of their pressing personal concerns and project an image of confidence. They do not, of course, want the priest to pretend he is divine nor do they wish him to act hypocritically or coolly aloof. But they do believe that suppression by the priest at the altar of his temporary worries or minor troubles in no way compromises integrity. And, they insist, it does wonders for his wavering flock.

I tend to agree with this latter approach, as does Father Hovda.

> These are days and years when lots of us are nervous. Yet a president whose nervousness or nervous mannerisms betray a lack of assurance and confidence cannot serve the assembly well. Whatever inward feelings we may have, we owe it to the congregation to preside with all the poise we can muster. Whatever weakness we may feel, the time of celebration is not the time to make our weakness the burden of the community. Christians have a right to look for strength in the person who exercises the office of presidency.[5]

Chapter 9

PRESIDENT OF THE COMMUNITY

Not too many years ago mention of the priest as a president, as a celebrant who presides over the community of worshipers, raised eyebrows and even brought mocking remarks from veteran workers in the ministry. The terms "president" and "community" in a liturgical sense were then unfamiliar and a bit threatening, but no longer.

Official documents teach that "the Lord's Supper is the assembly or gathering together of the people of God, with a priest presiding, to celebrate the memorial of the Lord."[1] In its fifth chapter on the Arrangement and Decoration of Churches for the Eucharistic Celebration the General Instruction even specifies the nature and correct location of a priest's presidential seat. "The celebrant's chair should express his office of presiding over the assembly and of directing prayer. Thus the proper place. . . ."[2]

In this chapter we intend to examine briefly the notion of a eucharistic community and then explore the role of a president who leads it in worship.

Eucharistic Community

Pope Paul VI's revised Roman Missal contains a succinct, but clear and comprehensive description of God's People gathered at the altar.

> In the celebration of Mass the faithful are a holy people, a chosen race, a royal priesthood, giving thanks to the Father and offering the victim and themselves not only through the hands of the priest but also with him. They should make this clear by their deep sense of religion and their charity to everyone who shares in the celebration.
>
> Any appearance of individualism or division should be avoided, since they are all brothers in the sight of the one Father.
>
> They should become one in hearing the word of God, joining in prayers and song, and in the common offering of sacrifice and sharing of the Lord's table. This unity is especially evident in the common postures and actions observed by the faithful.[3]

These concepts, especially the fundamental People of God notion, rest upon a developing realization over the last three decades of the intimate connection between the secular "assembly duly summoned" of Athens, the "Qahal Yahweh" or "the Assembly of Yahweh" in Old Testament times, and the "Church" of the new covenant.

In ancient Greece, heralds formally called together in the name of the civic authority all the people for a meeting on some matter of importance. Once summoned, these individuals became, as it were, a moral personality, listened to official remarks concerning their welfare, and took communal action in response. Similarly, the Qahal Yahweh convoked at the Holy City heard, as the people of Israel, their King's words and gave a formal answer to them. In New Testament times, the Apostles considered themselves as heralds of Israel's King, calling together by Jesus' Word the new people of God throughout the whole world and conveying to them the message of good news which this same Word wished to teach them. The preaching of these

Apostles came to be called a "proclamation" (*kerygma*) and was from the beginning associated with the idea of church, congregation, or assembly (*ecclesia*).[4]

Father Louis Bouyer draws these historical points together and relates them to the liturgy in his classic study, *Liturgical Piety*.

> The liturgy in its unity and in its perfection is to be seen as *the meeting of God's People called together in convocation by God's Word through the apostolic ministry, in order that the People, consciously united together, may hear God's Word itself in Christ, may adhere to that Word by means of the prayer and praise amid which the Word is proclaimed, and so seal by the Eucharistic sacrifice the Covenant which is accomplished by the same Word.*[5]

These ideas sound very beautiful, historically sound, and theologically correct, but are quite divorced from present reality. Certainly the deacon preaching peace in suburbia found his audience not a community consciously united together, but an assembly of deeply divided individuals. James Hitchcock, associate professor of history at Saint Louis University, would not be surprised by that Mother's Day eruption in a suburban parish. For him such a split between people simply confirms his more universal, but grim analysis of the contemporary scene. "All the communities we have known—churches, universities, neighborhoods, even families—seem to be in a state of collapse."[6]

Hitchcock, who blames the liturgical reform for much of our malaise, believes "the central crisis of the Church is really the breakdown of community, the diminishing sense Catholics now have that they really do share a unique identity and distinctive values."[7] Nor does he hold great hope for the future.

> There is little possibility of real Catholic community in the foreseeable future, although certain traditional-minded groups will huddle together, rather unsatisfactorily. For other individuals, however, to be a Catholic in anything approaching the traditional sense — which is so far the only

distinctive sense — will require lonely resolution and the endurance of isolation. Perhaps community will re-emerge at some future time, but one cannot expect it.[8]

I, for one, am not so pessimistic. Community is a loose term and an elusive goal as persons in communes, members of floating parishes, and reformers of parochial structures will understand. Must we have perfect community before worshiping together, or will good liturgy help mold better communities? Does the liturgy build community or presuppose, then express it? That debate has been raging for endless hours. It seems to me that each side has an insight to contribute. A warm, human, interacting assembly of people quite likely will worship much more effectively than a large, impersonal, unconnected crowd of individuals. At the same time persons who participate in a parish with carefully planned and properly executed Sunday Masses may walk away at least occasionally with a greater, although more or less conscious, awareness of what it is to be and to live as a Christian. The frequency of that occurrence, the intensity of this understanding no doubt will vary, and consciousness of it as well, but the growth cannot be denied.

The General Instruction sees the parish as something of a microcosm. "Mass celebrated by any community is important, but especially the parish community which represents the universal Church at a given time and place. This is particularly true of Mass on the Lord's day."[9] The parish does offer a panorama of the human community. Young and old, married and single, progressive and conservative, Democrats and Republicans, doves and hawks, black and white and brown — the mix basically is the same, although exact proportions vary according to particular circumstances. This tremendous diversity offers an often discouraging and always taxing challenge for those in charge of worship. Perhaps, however, the real witness of the Church today is showing how Christians, wide apart on many issues, still can close ranks in love, learn to live with others who differ, agree on the core of Christ's message, and join in common worship.

The Missal gives practical suggestions for attaining this objective. The purpose of the Introductory Rites, for example, "is to help the assembled people make themselves a worshiping community and to prepare them for listening to God's word and celebrating the eucharist."[10] We have talked already in this context about the value of a priest's greeting before Mass. A rousing song, prolonged enough to stir the people (not abruptly cut off after one verse), can also lift them out of their lethargy and continue that process of fashioning a community.

The official text states: "a common posture, as a sign which both expresses and fosters the inner spirit and purpose of the community, ought to be observed by all."[11] No liturgist seeks return to a formalism, a correct performance of the external gesture, a sitting, standing, kneeling at appropriate moments, without internal appreciation of what these gestures symbolize. In reaction to pure externalism some say it is of little consequence, for instance, whether the congregation stands or kneels during the Eucharistic Prayer or at the dismissal blessing. It is and it isn't. As long as a community clearly understands both the what and the why, then common posture promotes good liturgy. But failure to establish agreed patterns causes confusion and hinders community worship. Guests at a wedding (especially those who are not Roman Catholic) will fail to appreciate the ceremony's beauty, if they feel uncomfortable with and uninformed about the proper posture for these situations. On the other hand, if the celebrant gently explains when to stand, when to sit, when to kneel, those present can forget the mechanics and concentrate on the service itself.

The rite of peace is another illustration of concrete measures in the General Instruction designed to build community. "Before they share in the same bread the people express their love for one another and beg for peace and unity in the Church and with all mankind."[12] Initial attempts to introduce the peace sign met with resistance in some parts and created friction rather than harmony. Careful catechesis and prudent pulpit direction, however, can gradually win over the hesitant to this gesture which has great potential as a means of opening people to each other.

On the Sunday after that Mother's Day disturbance, a different preacher spoke about love, community, and acceptance of people as persons. He explained the sign of peace and encouraged parishioners, if they so desired, to exchange this gesture at the designated time. Not a word was mentioned of the preceding week's turbulence, but everyone caught the inference and most overcame their natural reluctance, turned to their neighbors and passed a greeting of peace. There was no artificiality on that day, no routine use of externals. I think the parish grew a little as a community.

The Celebrant as President

The General Instruction to the Roman Missal summarizes rather well the functions of a celebrant as president of the eucharistic community.

> As president of the congregation, the priest gives instructions and words of introduction and conclusion indicated within the rite itself, proclaims the word of God, and gives the final blessing. He may also very briefly introduce the Mass of the day (before the celebration begins), comment on the liturgy of the word (before the readings), and the eucharistic prayer (before the preface); he may give concluding comments before the dismissal.
>
> Among the parts assigned to the priest, the eucharistic prayer has precedence; it is the high point of the celebration. Next are the prayers: the opening prayer or collect, the prayer over the gifts, and the prayer after communion. The priest, presiding in the person of Christ, addresses the prayers to God in the name of the entire assembly and thus they are called presidential prayers.
>
> As president the priest prays in the name of the whole community. Besides this, he prays at times in his own name so that he may exercise his ministry. These prayers are said quietly with attention and devotion.[13]

These are very lucid instructions, but they generally indicate to the priest only the when and the what, not the how. We need to plunge a bit deeper and pursue this matter of attitude or approach, discuss the how, the manner in which an effective president actually performs these tasks.

Not as a dictator. The Liturgical Conference published, in 1964, *Priest's Guide to Parish Worship*, a handy manual on celebration. Its description of a dictatorial president bears repeating for those of us who live in the seventies.

> The dictator dominates; he controls by doing everything himself or by delegating only insignificant functions and insisting that these be carried out in strict conformity to his own personal tastes and according to his whims. The dictator is officious. He believes — perhaps quite unconsciously — that all others exist only to admire and add luster to his performance. The priest-dictator at Mass is marked by affectations and eccentricities, by irritation when some hapless server or choir member ruins "his" Mass. The priest-dictator destroys community worship because he destroys the community. He reduces those who have come to participate with him in the eucharistic action to less than their personal dignity by throttling their initiative. His people sense that he would not welcome their joining him as adults playing an adult role. And so they relapse into the respectful attention of the disinterested or the bored.[14]

The dictator attempts to compel a response, the true president seeks to elicit one. The latter knows that grace works best in a climate of freedom and knows people will not be pushed, especially in modern times. He recognizes that they jealously guard their personal rights and respond only when treated as adults, as mature individuals, as unique beings each with a special dignity. Barking at people because they won't sing or imposing the sign of peace without regard for their sensitivities just won't do.

More and more dioceses, to illustrate, now follow a policy of flexibility in determining the age for first confession and Communion. The training of children and the judgment as to their fitness for either sacrament is left in most instances to the parents. So, too, fewer Catholic schools herd their flocks over to church on the Thursday before First Friday for confession. In these and other areas, recognition of the need for personal initiative and faith in liturgy, for an atmosphere of free choice and the absence of enforced conformity has, fortunately, diminished some of our overbearing ways.

But the president should not be an abdicator either.

> Abdication on the part of the leader is equally disruptive of any community action. Once again any true community is destroyed, this time because all are invited to indulge themselves as individuals rather than to fulfill their proper roles for the good of the community as a whole. The priest who has abdicated his role as president gives no encouragement and no guidance, refuses the difficult task of making things run smoothly. His people become insecure. No one is sure just what his part is or how he should do it. The diffident and retiring find themselves pushed aside and gradually become silent. The more confident and determined rapidly become soloists. This is the situation in which the choir begrudges hymns sung by the people, the people complain of the impossible selections made by the choir, and the organist frowns equally upon both.[15]

The celebrant's task, then, is to pull all things together. That function, since it affects different persons performing different duties on different days, involves a certain dynamism and requires an ability to make decisions on the spot. He must, for example, estimate when a period of silence is productive and prolong it and when the moment of quiet has become destructive and end it. He needs in those cases to judge when the tension of silent prayer has a creative effect on the community and when it is beginning to wear on the congregation. No preconceived, computer-like, rigid rules can determine that. Only a living, alert president of the assembly.

An abdicator might wish to sing during Communion time, forgetting that his omission of the individual "Body of Christ" deprives someone of an opportunity to verbalize personal faith. We might also believe unison recitation of the eucharistic prayer by everyone achieves full participation, overlooking the division of roles essential in liturgy and cutting thereby his own presidential throat.

The model liturgical president in some ways brings to mind the master of ceremonies from older days. The latter was expected to know every person's part and weld a number of individual performers into one smooth and flowing service. Today's celebrant needs to understand his own function and accomplish it well, to know the responsibilities of others and facilitate their handling of these roles, and, above all, to unite the entire community in the Lord's Supper so "that the ministers and the faithful may take their own proper part in it and thus gain its fruits more fully."[16]

Chapter 10

COMMUNICATION I
READING

Several years ago the Oakland Liturgical Commission surveyed parishes of its diocese to determine the effectiveness of priests and lectors in communicating a message to the congregation. The dismal results, reported originally in the October, 1967 issue of *Living Worship* and summarized by Father Hovda in the *Worship* article we have already cited, suggest that all was not liturgically well in churches of the San Francisco Bay area. Unfortunately, the quality of official reading at worship in other parts of the nation was, I would judge, not any better and possibly much worse.

The survey noted:

      Priest's audibility from the altar — 20% effective,
                                     80% ineffective;

      From the pulpit — 85% effective,
                 15% ineffective;

      Lector's audibility — 60% effective;
                  40% ineffective;

> His reading, delivery impact, and relative preparedness –
> 20% effective,
> 80% ineffective.

We can hope some improvement has been made in the overall communication picture since the days of that study. This may very well be true, but the General Instruction of the Roman Missal continues to urge that all lectors, clerical or lay, have the talent and training necessary to convey effectively God's Word in liturgical celebrations.

> Readers should be qualified and carefully prepared so that the reading will develop in the faithful an appreciation of Scripture.[2]
> Texts should be said in a clear, loud voice, whether by the priest or by the ministers or by everyone. The tone of voice should correspond to the nature of the text, such as a reading, a prayer, an instruction, an acclamation, or a song; the tone also depends on the form of celebration and the solemnity of the assembly. The characteristics of different languages and peoples should be considered.[3]

This same document gives us the theological reasons why those in charge of planning community worship must insist on a careful reading of biblical texts and other passages.

> In the readings, God speaks to his people of the mystery of salvation and nourishes their spirit; Christ is present through his word.[4]
> In the readings the treasures of the bible are opened to the people; this is the table of God's word .[5]
> The liturgy indicates that the reading of the gospel should be done with reverence; it is distinguished from the other readings by special marks of honor. A special minister proclaims it, preparing himself by a blessing or prayer. By standing to hear the reading and by their acclamations, the people recognize and acknowledge that Christ is present and speaking to them. Marks of honor are also given to the gospel book itself.[6]

The General Instruction also clearly distinguishes between the celebrant's role and the duties of a lector. While the priest may, on occasions of necessity, fulfill the tasks of a reader, the revised liturgy assigns the lector a proper function all his own.

> Whether he is a layman or a cleric, the reader has his own proper function in the eucharistic celebration and should exercise this even though ministers of a higher rank are present. Except for the gospel—and at those times when a subdeacon is present, the epistle—he proclaims all the scripture readings. If there is no chanter for the psalm, the reader may also sing or read the psalm between the readings.[7]

Finally, in these days of the liberation movement for women, the following words may prove of interest.

> When a qualified man is not available, the conference of bishops may permit a woman to proclaim the readings prior to the gospel, while standing outside the sanctuary.[8]

The National Conference of Catholic Bishops at its November 1969, meeting approved this proposal of women lectors for the United States. The terms seem terribly restrictive, especially to concerned feminists, but canonical interpretations of the phrase "outside the sanctuary" remove part of the limitation. A comparison of this text with an earlier Vatican commentary on the place of women choir members in the sanctuary leads us to conclude that female readers and leaders may stand in the sanctuary (*sanctuarium*) as long as they do not remain in the area immediately about the altar in which the celebrating clergy function (*presbyterium*). That would appear to allow distaff lectors the freedom of proclaiming scriptural texts from either lectern or pulpit depending on the most satisfactory procedure in a given parish or community.[9]

Moreover, it seems to me that the clause, "when a qualified man is not available," also should be interpreted quite liberally. These guidelines for liturgical celebrations provided in the General Instruction hope above all to encourage properly prepared and well-executed worship services. Competent readers are indispensable for that type of good liturgy. Competence appears as the key word in this discussion, competence in reading God's word. Sex should not stand as the determining factor; an ability to proclaim the sacred text ought to be the one qualifying criterion. Better to employ a woman who reads well than a man who does the job poorly; and, in my view, better to use a priest for all of the scriptural excerpts, if no layman or laywoman in the worshiping community can at the present stage of renewal adequately communicate the meaning of these passages.

Cleric or lay person, man or woman, the lector in liturgy should, as I mentioned, possess adequate natural talents and have received suitable training. Once again, if we accept the recent study of a speech scholar, our past history leaves much to be desired, particularly with regard to the kind of preparatory programs available for seminarians, priests, and the laity. In 1969, Robert J. Wesley, chairman of the speech and theatre department at Salisbury State College in Maryland, submitted "A Study of Instruction for Liturgical Reading in Roman Catholic Diocesan Seminaries in the United States" as his dissertation for a doctor of philosophy degree at Wayne State University. He notes in his conclusions that courses for oral interpretation in diocesan seminaries are generally nonexistent or second-rate, the staff poorly qualified (almost 50% of the faculty who teach speech hold no graduate degrees in the subject), and the resources (audiovisual machines and reference libraries) insufficient for the task.[10] Moreover, he learned in his research of few well-organized and thorough training programs for lay lectors.

There are, however, signs of progress. The Atlanta Archdiocesan Liturgical Commission in the last year sponsored several workshops for priests of the diocese on the art of communicating. Each session involved a small number of participants — twelve or fourteen at the most — and a full day of work in a local Protestant radio-television center. The priests performed before videotape cameras, watched themselves, heard criticisms from confreres, and worked to improve style and delivery. One pastor, somewhat skeptical in the beginning and reluctant to come, walked away a believer. "I've learned," he said, "more about myself and about communicating in fifteen minutes on tape than I have in the past ten years of priesthood." The costs to the Atlanta commission ran high (about $350 per day for studio rental and professional consultant), but members judge this educational project for the clergy by far the best program they have sponsored during these days of liturgical renewal.

The Peoria diocese, as another illustration, recently invited representatives from the Christian Preaching Conference in St. Louis to conduct a similar session for lectors and celebrants. Priests spent Friday afternoon and evening, laymen all day Saturday, working with Sony videotape equipment. Less expensive than the Atlanta arrangement, planners nevertheless deemed it most successful although Father George Remm, the Liturgical Commission's executive secretary, felt that the great number who participated overtaxed the facilities and diminished the program's value.

Training courses in oral interpretation on a diocesan or regional level could resolve a sticky pastoral problem. Parishes quite desperately need good readers—Sunday liturgies simply fail without them—but the pastor also must deal with sensitive human beings who are or would like to be lectors, yet lack the fundamental talents required. A more impersonal, multiparish project for the instruction and evaluation of lay readers would help provide qualified personnel in this area and at the same moment discourage well-intentioned, but inadequately endowed individuals.

Clarke mentions some of the characteristics essential for a potential lector: he should be audible, able to make sense of what is being read, have an ease of pronunciation, know how to pace himself, how to stand still at the lectern, how to follow the printed page without being its slave.[11]

The director of a training institute for readers, more detached from candidates than the local priest, can judge these qualities with greater objectivity. He likewise can reject unsuitable prospects with fewer hurt feelings. We anticipate that other diocesan liturgical commissions in the country will follow the lead of Atlanta and Peoria and assume an ever-increasing role in this vital aspect of liturgical reform.

Carefully prepared passages, suitably qualified lectors, proper-ly trained readers go totally to waste when the person at a lectern or in the pulpit must cope with a poor microphone and a malfunctioning public-address system. Conscientious preparation and delivery of a homily or scriptural text drains something from a man. When he discovers his words were not even heard because of dead spots in the church, when whining feedback interrupts the flow of his message at a dramatic and crucial point, when he learns the sacristan forgot to turn the correct switches beforehand, he is mad, frustrated, discouraged. Listeners in the pews probably don't react so strongly to the interference; they try for a while to follow the unclear presentation, then give up and wander off into their own thought worlds. This takes little effort and is less irritating.

One longs for a day when parishes will be smaller and churches so acoustically engineered that no artificial amplifying devices will be needed at all. The Church of the Most Holy Rosary in Lowellville, Ohio, already makes that dream a reality. A priest in the pulpit or at the altar speaks naturally, normally, and any one of the 400-plus congregation can easily see him and hear his words. No microphones are necessary here, no unsightly cords, and no uneven, fading, garbled phrases either. Poor communication in this parish is a priest's or lector's fault, not the microphone's.

Lowellville, unfortunately, stands as an exception. In many, if not most parishes, we have no choice but to employ microphones and a public-address system. Commitment to high quality liturgy means, therefore, that we seek out professional advice, don't skimp on money, and install the best available unit. Makeshift setups and amateur volunteer servicemen betray, I fear, a preoccupation with costs. To spend dimes on worship and dollars on other parochial needs spells disaster in my mind, or at least poor value judgments. Once more, certain practical considerations flow from the priorities of Vatican II and Küng's notion about the Church ("But Christ is above all present and active in the worship of the congregation. . ."[12]). A superior communication system in the church is one of them.

Whatever our desires and expectations for smaller, microphoneless structures in the future, we must deal with "here and now" circumstances and make maximum use of existing public-address systems. Clarke offers a few suggestions. "Keep microphone coverage as flexible as possible; have an adjustable amplifier; employ the smallest possible microphones; don't let the 'mike' hide or divide your face; avoid too high a volume (picks up page-turning and breathing sounds, fosters 'feedback' reactions); never cough or blow into the microphone (the former makes a deafening noise, the latter damages the instrument); watch too much sibilance (a 'mike' is extremely sensitive to the 's'); practice beforehand; be careful to keep intake of breath silent; forget the microphone is there."[13]

Our remarks up to this point have touched on the need for qualified readers, the type of training programs required to provide such lectors, and the necessity of a suitable communication system in every church. We move on to make a few comments on the "how" of good reading.

In November 1964, the Bishops' Commission on the Liturgical Apostolate prepared certain recommendations for "Reading and Praying in the Vernacular." They form, in my opinion, the best, the most succinct statement of general principles for "Reading the Word of God" we now have in print. For this reason I quote from them at some length.

> All Scripture readings are to be proclamations, not mere recitations. Lectors and priests should approach the public reading of the Bible with full awareness that it is their honored task to render the official proclamation of the revealed Word of God to His assembled holy people. The character of this reading is such that it must convey that special reverence which is due the Sacred Scriptures above all other words.
>
> 1. It is of fundamental importance that the reader communicate the fullest meaning of the passage. Without exaggerated emphasis or affectation, he must convey the particular significance of those words, phrases, clauses, or sentences which constitute the point being made. Careful phrasing and inflection are necessary to enable the listener to follow every thought and the relationship among them. Patterns of speech, especially monotonous patterns of speech, must be avoided, and the pattern of thought in the

text must be adhered to. The message in all its meaning must be earnestly communicated.

2. The manner of speaking and tone of voice should be clear and firm, never indifferent or uncertain. The reader should not draw attention to himself either by being nervous and awkward or by being obviously conscious of a talent for dramatic reading. It is the message that should be remembered, not the one who reads it. The voice should be reverent without being unctuous, loud without shouting, authoritative without being offensive or overbearing. The pace must be geared to understanding—never hurried, never dragged.

3. By his voice, attitude, and physical bearing, the reader should convey the dignity and sacredness of the occasion. His role is that of a herald of the Word of God, his function to provide a meaningful encounter with that living Word. Perfection in this mission may not always be achieved, but it must always and seriously be sought.[14]

To conclude this particular section on "how to read" and the entire chapter on communication through reading, I summarize a number of practical tips culled from Clarke's book, personal experience, and pastoral observation.[15]

1. *Read a text over aloud, five times beforehand.* In doing so, try to discern the flow of action, the trend of thoughts. Broken down in this fashion, the reader can, during the public reading, employ pauses to convey the fullest meaning of each passage. To be honest, this writer has taken the time and trouble on few Saturday evenings in the past six months, and practically never on weekdays. I wonder how many priests (and lay lectors) are guilty of similar neglect and seldom practice in advance. When a layman runs to the sacristy at the last minute on Sunday, nervously looks for the appropriate excerpts, and tries quickly to read through them before Mass begins, I have strong doubts about careful and repeated rehearsals at home. Our record as priest-readers probably is not much better, but this ideal of pre-reading rests on a solid foundation and certainly should enhance the quality of liturgies.

2. *Don't print (or have printed) in participation aids the actual texts of scriptural readings.* Some priests and publishers will, I know, react violently to this suggestion. (They *have* vocally during lectures over the last year.) But my personal conviction about it grows daily. Communication through reading entails more than a verbal, audio presentation. The face and body and hands contribute. When a congregation buries itself in a missalette or leaflet missal or missal and never looks at the lector, this total dimension of the communicating process is immediately lost. I grant that we have a problem with the deaf, with poor readers, and with inadequate public-address systems. I also admit that it is better for persons to read along with the lector rather than to hear little and understand less. Still these are moments designed for people to listen, not to read. Attentive and perceptive listening, I agree, may seem foreign to American traditions.

Furthermore, it probably will take years to train competent readers, install suitable amplifying systems, and develop in congregations an ability to listen well. Printing the biblical texts (and also the Eucharistic Prayers as we shall note in our next chapter) indeed may serve as a needed crutch through this transition period, but it should not be accepted as the model procedure and in truth probably retards the liturgical progress of both lector and hearer.

3. *Clearly indicate the book from which an excerpt has been taken and carefully pronounce proper nouns, including obscure Old Testament names.* The audience will very likely remember none of these seemingly inconsequential items. However, if the lector slides over or slurs them, a certain frustration unconsciously arises within the listener which ultimately will distract him. And once a hearer's attention slips, the reader must fight furiously to regain it.

4. *Never read while the congregation is in motion.* After the opening prayer has been completed, a lector should allow ample time for the audience to sit, cough, look around, squirm, turn pages, and become comfortable. The priest or deacon ought to follow a parallel pattern before starting the Gospel. A silent

pause until everyone appears ready to listen attracts attention, and even gains the ear of those less disposed. Similarly, to pause for a few beats after the introduction aids in focusing a congregation's thoughts on the core of each text.

5. *Begin firmly.* This sets the scene, establishes a context, creates a climate.

6. *Remember that the pause is generally the reader's most powerful tool.* It can convey a shift in the movement of a story and a change in the writer's thought pattern. It can mark off direct speech and heighten tension in preparation for an important sentence. It can give words an opportunity to reach people's ears and be absorbed by them. The pause, however, is a delicate instrument, albeit a potent one. It should be longer in a large building than in a small one, shorter for 25 persons than for 2,500. It should be frequent, but not too frequent; brief, but not too brief; extended, but not too extended.

7. *Stand still*—for the same reasons we mentioned in the preceding chapter.

8. *Keep your place.* I find it helpful to use one finger on the page as a reference, permitting extended eye contact without fear of losing my spot in the passage. Clarke discourages this practice and argues, "It should not be necessary to follow the text with the fingers. This is distracting for the listener. The best cure for this habit is constant practice in reading out loud."[16] Our minor disagreement should not cloud concurrence on the root issue—look as often as possible at the congregation, but without forgetting where you are in the text. Whatever a reader decides about his finger as an aid in following the selection, the hands should otherwise rest lightly on the lectern. Hands tightly clasped before the stomach may look strange and awkward from the main part of the church.

9. *Check the building's size.* A larger church requires longer pauses, more precise enunciation, a slower pace, greater attention to the vicissitudes of a microphone system. The voice in these structures must bear the brunt of the burden since facial expressions and even bodily gestures will be indiscernible for

many in the congregation. A smaller church obviously offers a more inviting setting for oral interpretation, but here, too, each lector must evaluate the situation and judge what kind of volume, pause, and pace will best serve his needs.

10. *Avoid shuffling papers.* This advice pertains more to a homily than to the scriptural readings, and more to radio broadcasting than to pulpit oratory. Whenever the reader or preacher must follow a printed text of several pages, he should see beforehand that they are unstapled, loose or free, and can be shifted as silently as possible. Such a minor matter is not so minor on radio when unnecessary and unpleasant noises can seriously distract listeners and detract from the program's impact.

Chapter 11

COMMUNICATION II
PREACHING

It's not easy to move people or change their lives. Men travel along in something of a rut, pushed into conversions and forced to change patterns of life only by a crisis from within or from without. Priests should not, therefore, expect to transform every parishioner each Sunday by a few words from the pulpit. But we do. We question the value of weekly sermons, grow discouraged when carefully prepared homilies apparently stir no response, feel frustrated over the seeming lack of growth in our listeners.

Personal growth and conversion and change are difficult movements to measure. Generally individual improvement is an imperceptible, inch-by-inch kind of struggle. Critical moments demanding radical decisions involve considerable pain or trauma, and, it is true, send us substantially forward (or backward). But these crises, while not uncommon, occur infrequently in the average man's life. We work out our salvation more through a humdrum existence, day in and day out duties, unspectacular responsibilities.

The celebrant in the Sabbath pulpit faces a few persons preoccupied with crises. Most of his hearers, however, are simply caught up in the everyday routine of work, home, and family. The former may be tremendously influenced by his remarks since their turbulent state leaves them very open to sensitive comments on the substantive issues of life and living. The latter, more at peace and quite content with their situation, will not, really cannot, psychologically, react in such strong fashion to a sermon however superb. Yet even these, the "average" worshipers, can be moved, touched, motivated by a good homily. The question is, I suppose, how the preacher brings this off.

How does he cause tears to flow? How does he elicit a quiet smile, a knowing nod, an affectionate glance? How does he hold distracted modern man in rapt attention? How does he keep hundreds of people absolutely still and silent without nervous coughing or impatient wiggling? How does he provoke warm handshakes of appreciation after Mass, unsolicited letters of praise, "very inspiring sermon" comments? How, in a word, does he "get to people"?

Rev. Charles A. Curran, writing for *Guide* magazine a few years ago, explored these questions in his "The Psychology of Audience Reaction: Personal Change Through Sermons."[1] A reprint of an address by the same author given to the Catholic Homiletic Society, the article maintains:

> Through psychological research in counseling and psychotherapy, we have learned that people are most helped to make personal changes in conduct when they are aided to take counsel with themselves and interrelate the information they are receiving with their own inner world of personalized singularity.[2]

Father Curran applies this technical principle to the homily.

> We rather suggest to our sermon audience some deeply human theme and allow each one's own introspection to develop his uniquely personal variations and details.[3]

In effect the author says that sermons which motivate people need to speak about feelings and concerns and situations they do now or have personally experienced in the past. Inwardly the hearer must say, "I felt that way once," or "I am worried about that very thing," or "I was in that same predicament." Simultaneously he shakes his head in agreement and mutters approval to himself. The speaker, in this man's view, is talking about something real, relevant, personal. And he listens.

Curran describes Jesus' effective use of this technique in our Lord's parable of the Prodigal Son. Through the medium of a story Christ speaks about a variety of common, deeply shared human experiences: the conflicting feelings of a father who loves his son, wants him to stay at home, and foresees potential ruin if he leaves, yet knows this young man must be free, must leave, must make his own decisions for better or for worse; the deep guilt of a person who has wasted much, hurt himself and presumably injured others in the process; the loneliness of a sinner who now wanders alone and unloved; the fear of admitting one's mistake to those we love, the anxiety of crawling back to God, the doubt that he and they will forgive; the tendency to wallow in remorse or self-pity and not to forgive oneself; the inexpressible joy of regaining peace, receiving forgiveness, and being able to start anew.

Every listener in Jesus' times and ours knows at least some of these conflicts and has experienced many of these emotions. He identifies with them. As the parable unfolds he turns over in his mind similar past events which happened to *him*, previous moments when *he* felt guilt, fear, loneliness, earlier occasions when a sense of peace and forgiveness returned to *him*. For the hearer who at that very instant feels any of these sentiments, the story can carry an overwhelming impact. But at the very least a sermon with such content does strike home and will undoubtedly "get" to the congregation.

Some of Christ's parables (e.g., the woman taken in adultery, Mary Magdalene, the good thief, "Whatever you do to one of these the least of my brothers. . .") on their own and with very little explanation speak to contemporary man. Others, like the mustard seed or fig tree comparisons, do not work so well. They require background exegesis and imaginative application to current events.

The point, then, is that powerful homilies must begin where the hearers are. The preacher needs to ask himself, "What is on the mind of this congregation; what are these people thinking about, worrying about; what current events have them preoccupied right now in the pews before me?" The deacon we mentioned earlier, for example, understandably distressed by developments in Cambodia, may have badly misjudged the temperament of parishioners, or the majority of them, on that explosive Mother's Day. These people hoped to hear some inspirational words about motherhood and the Blessed Mother and love; they felt "uptight" enough about tension in the nation and simply were not in a mood to hear controversial words from the altar. On a different Sunday the reaction might have been less hostile, more receptive.

In a similar vein, the priest must always be willing to discard an earlier prepared sermon when sudden critical occurrences change the entire climate of a parish community. I am thinking, by way of illustration, about the dark days after John F. Kennedy's assassination. In those years many dioceses, including ours, followed a syllabus for preaching which covered nearly every Sunday of the year. The topic assigned and outlined for that fateful weekend in November was mixed marriages, a subject normally of significant interest to any congregation. However, in parishes where a preacher ignored the turn of events and adhered to the diocesan program, and many did, the homily seemed incongruous, totally irrelevant to the heavy, somber thoughts and feelings of Americans who were in mourning, tearfully glued to television sets and deeply shaken by what was to be the first of several such tragedies.

Alertness to the surrounding environment or atmosphere presupposes, of course, that the celebrant is "plugged in," as it were, to the contemporary world. It means he reads the daily newspaper, scans *Newsweek* and *Life*, listens to his car radio, watches television. The late talk-shows of Carson and Cavett, the best-selling paperback novel, the year's ten best movies all tell us something about modern man and can serve as a springboard for sermons. The priest who reads *only* these things, listens *only* to these programs, watches *only* these shows naturally will not be in much of a position to shed some divine light on human problems or evaluate daily events in terms of the gospel.

He has allowed himself to be swallowed up in secularity. But a preacher who maintains the proper perspective may indeed combine something of the divine-human qualities in his homilies which characterized the style of Christ's preaching.

The *topic* or *content*, then, forms the first and essential ingredient of a good sermon. The Sacred Congregation of Rites issued an instruction in 1964 outlining preliminary steps for the implementation of the Liturgy Constitution. It defined in rather general terms both the nature and content of a homily.

> By a homily from the sacred text is understood an explanation either of some aspect of the readings from holy Scripture or of another text from the Ordinary or Proper of the Mass of the day, taking into account the mystery which is being celebrated and the particular needs of the hearers.[4]

The General Instruction speaks in similar words:

> The homily is strongly recommended as a integral part of the liturgy and as a necessary source of nourishment for the Christian life. It should develop some point of the readings or of another text from the Ordinary or the Mass of the day. The homilist should keep in mind the mystery that is being celebrated and the needs of the particular community.[5]

A preacher needs, therefore, to begin with the event, the mystery, the scriptural excerpts and apply it to the "here and now" situation of his congregation. A phrase by phrase exegesis of the biblical reading is neither required nor desired. And a theological explanation or a catechetical instruction alone, divorced from application to the contemporary scene and without reference to the Eucharistic celebration, leaves something lacking. The homilist assumes the role, and it is a formidable one at that, of a synthesizer, of a speaker who can fuse the eternal, inspired words of God with the present, pressing concerns of men. He must somehow show we worship a living Lord of salvation history, an Emmanuel, a Creator dwelling with us who is both interested and active in our lives. What does this God say in today's Mass about today's problems? That is the preacher's goal in a nutshell. He should raise real questions, air them, expose them to Christ's principles. It is not for him to supply tailor-made solutions or instant answers to the hopelessly complex issues of death, failure, fear, pessimism, hatred, sickness, sin, confidence, forgiveness, love, joy, life, peace, happiness. But, instead, he only brings these basic matters out in the open, sheds some divine light on them, and allows each individual to sift the message and judge how it fits his own personal circumstances.

The good news commandment of love, to offer an example, often occurs in the Sunday series of biblical readings. On one of these occasions, a preacher might bring into the pulpit *Time* magazine for February 14, 1969. An article in that issue, "Hugh Hefner Faces Middle Age," finds the millionaire originator of *Playboy* a bit restless and melancholy as he recognizes that there are only so many years in which to do certain things. The idea of committed love in contrast to casual encounters now seems to hold appeal for Hefner. "You know," says Hef wistfully, "in the next ten years I would rather meet a girl and fall in love, and have her fall in love with me than make another hundred million dollars."[6] Stories or quotations like this quickly attract and hold attention. And with very little effort, the homilist can use such examples to drive home Christ's words about the nature and necessity of true love for Christian living and human happiness.

The content of a homily, therefore, should ideally integrate the mystery being celebrated, the needs of a particular community, and the atmosphere in which this congregation moves. But the *manner* in which this material is presented naturally affects the success of any homily.

To create the optimum sense of warmth and the spirit of mutual common concerns, Curran favors "a somewhat calm and conversational tone." He expands on this :

> The speaker depends on the speaking system to carry his words into the ear of each hearer. The speaker avoids those mannerisms that would perhaps take the hearer away from his own self-involved pondering on what the speaker is say-

ing. For the purpose we have in mind, the hearer is rather talking to himself, counseling himself even, through the voice of the speaker. The speaker therefore strives rather to lead and direct this deep personal meditation more than to attract attention to himself. His appeal, in so far as it is emotional, has a more suppressed and therefore intense quality in comparison with a more directly dramatic expression. It is more like the warm tone of deep sharing and understanding in the voice of a sensitive counselor.[7]

One can think of a few other practical pointers on this question of proper pulpit delivery.

1. *Don't read from a text.* A preacher seldom conveys the kind of sincerity, personal interest, and sympathetic involvement Curran advocates when he closely follows a written script. All of these qualities may well be present in the priest, but the congregation cannot catch his concern for them as persons because of his concentration on the papers before him. The type of preparation we will suggest at the end of this chapter should eliminate the need for such complete dependency upon word for word notes.

2. *Prepare your own homily.* It should be evident that "canned" sermons simply cannot include the local and immediate elements indispensable for effective preaching. They may stimulate the development of ideas and start trains of thought, but wholesale transfer of the latest *Homiletic and Pastoral Review* from rectory chair to church lectern spells disaster.

3. *Be brief.* I indicated earlier that I personally think the average parish congregation on Sunday morning has a maximum attention span of ten minutes. Clear, uncluttered, well-constructed homilies with one, two, or three points can make lasting impressions; lengthy, complicated, scholarly sermons will be hard to digest and easy to forget. The more a priest says, the less people remember.

4. *Never concentrate on one particular person.* If a preacher does this, the unfortunate individual will feel uncomfortable and even victimized by such centering of attention on him. On the

other hand, constantly roving eyes give the appearance of shiftiness, of a fear to look people straight in the face. Slowly turning to all parts of the church and dwelling on a slightly larger area than one person should keep the preacher from both pitfalls.

5. *Stand still.* Raymond Clarke in his *Sounds Effective* covers the point nicely:

> Stillness is vital for any speaker. If there is stillness then it is easy for full attention to be paid to the words without their being blunted by irrevelant movements. If a speaker is continually moving, the listener eventually ends by watching the movements rather than listening to what is said. The body should be still and quietly at ease, with the weight spread evenly over both feet.[8]

For special situations, e.g., children's Masses or dialogue homilies, this recommendation would understandably not apply. However, even in those cases nervous mannerisms or excessive wandering detracts from the message.

6. *Keep face up and voice clear.* The congregation which must strain to see and to hear the homilist soon grows weary and drops off into dreamland. Mumbled words destroy a sermon, and a hidden face weakens it.

7. *Beware of professional jargon, cliches, and repetition.* The superior preacher speaks of sublime ideas in simple terms. He avoids trying to impress with technical phrases ("thematic harmonization coupled with semi-continuous readings") and checks regularly by taping his talks for trite, repeated expressions ("Let us therefore. . .").

This writer recently delivered a long lecture on the average of once a week for a six-month period. However, only after watching a videotape of the address did he discover, much to his pained surprise, that he had slipped into a habit of using "And so" as a connective several dozen times in the talk.

8. *Follow Anglo-Saxon language patterns, not Latinisms.* Strive for short, direct sentence structure; employ hard words, not abstractions; use active, not passive voice of verbs. Avoid

adverbs and excessive modification. Prepare a homily to be heard, not read.

Bishop Fulton J. Sheen once described his seven steps of preparation for a sermon. The process started a week in advance when he selected the subject and did some background reading on it. During the next days he meditated on the topic and material, wrote and rewrote, then read his text aloud. In the middle of this preparation he purposely would do nothing for 24 hours on the talk. This allowed his mind to lie fallow, and on the following day he would resume work and finalize the script. That procedure, not in fact terribly time-consuming, permitted a slow buildup of ideas through the week. Moreover, it insured that the final product would be part of his very being, would be him. A priest who takes similar, gradual pains in preparing homilies will find a sermon deeply ingrained in his mind and heart, and will require little by way of notes to prompt him once in the pulpit.

This kind of prayerful preparation will, I believe, more likely occur when parishes with several priests operate on the rotating schedule for preaching I urged in Chapter 5. The man who ascends the pulpit at *all* Sunday Masses every two or three or four weeks should be more inclined to prepare with the care of a Bishop Sheen than the cleric who speaks only at his own Mass week after week.

The liturgical commissions for New York, Brooklyn, and Rockville Centre issued an excellent *Handbook for the Revised Roman Liturgy* when the new Order of Mass was published by the Holy See. Its section on the homily is especially valuable, and a sample from that booklet fittingly concludes this chapter on the celebrant's role as homilist.

> Homily preparation is one of the main occupations of the priest. It should be considered an integral and necessary part and aspect of his spiritual life. The priest is not only called to transmit the Gospel objectively; it is also his duty to do it subjectively, to put his heart into it, and to involve his entire person. The preparation for preaching, therefore, should involve time spent in exegesis of the pericopes and texts of the liturgy. It demands *prayer* over these texts. It

demands time for actual composition and some consideration of the style of delivery. In short, the preparation of the
Sunday homily holds a priority in his daily schedule.[9]

Chapter 12

COMMUNICATION III PROCLAIMING

Dr. G. B. Harrison, former professor of English at the University of Michigan, retired and residing in the Southwest, today spends much of his time at work as a translator-advisor-consultant for the International Committee on English in the Liturgy. After ICEL versions of the *Ordo Missae*, marriage, and baptismal rites received approval from the American hierarchy and other English-speaking episcopal conferences, he wrote an article for *America* outlining the recent efforts of this organization. In a concluding paragraph, however, Harrison directed some warning words to priests who use these translations in liturgical celebrations.

> Manuals of celebration used to provide aids for the sacrament of penance, lists of sins that might have been overlooked since one's last confession: "Have you committed murder? If so, how often? You need not mention names." There should be similar aids for the clergy, including a section on the performance as a celebrant. "Have I always and carefully read over the Mass of the day before entering the

sanctuary? Have I chosen the second or third Eucharistic Prayer because it is shorter than the first or the fourth? Have I been fully conscious that the response of the congregation depends on how skillfully I lead them?" I mention this matter because those who are interested in the liturgy in English are acutely conscious of the way it is said.[1]

We have repeatedly stressed in this book the importance of a celebrant's role for excellent liturgy. Talk about worship as an action of the Christian community, efforts to involve the laity in Sunday Mass, formation of parish committees to plan weekly liturgies—these things are all well and good, but fortunately or unfortunately the success or failure of a service heavily depends on the performance of the priest who leads a celebration. He must communicate, get a message across to his listeners, convey an idea or message or conviction. Preaching forms part of that communicating process; reading biblical passages during the liturgy of the word is another aspect of it. But we cannot restrict the celebrant's opportunities for communication to these verbal presentations alone. He speaks in many ways—with his eyes, through facial expressions and bodily gestures, by his very being. A priest proclaims the good news of salvation in the liturgy by sight and sound, he communicates when the congregation recognizes him as a person who believes, a person who prays, a person who really means what he says or does as a leader of worship.

The 1970 Atlanta Congress on Worship featured Miss Christiane Brusselman, a renowned catechist from the Universities of Louvain in Belgium and Fordham in New York, as one of the main speakers. In her lecture, "Prayer—The Need We Feel," she made some incisive comments about meaningful gestures.

Children, the young, men of our time fear the artificial, fear that which is unnatural, strained. Man today distrusts the formula simply because it *is* a formula. He distrusts the gesture if it is simply a gesture. He hates to be regimented; he feels diminished, feels that his whole, total human powers are kind of killed and restrained. And these are legitimate fears, I find, for the modern Christian.

Instead, the Christian of our classrooms, the Christian of our communities seeks for that which is spontaneous, tender, believing, direct. Man wants his action to be *his*, and in every activity he wants to renew his commitment to freedom. He just fears the superficial, and he yearns to commit himself to that which is really essential. Yes, he wants actions, attitudes and involvements that flow from the inner intention and inner disposition. He wants a personal and free commitment to life.

Words and gestures have this mysterious power of carrying out meaning, but because of this they also run the perpetual risk of losing meaning by a mindless use of them, and this is extremely important. I think, for instance, of the liturgy which is filled with gesture, but at times the routine and the habit have made us unaware of the meaning underlying the gesture.

The real Christian and the real person who wants to be fully human is the one who constantly *puts* into his gestures and into his words truth and meaning; he puts *himself* into a gesture.[2]

In Chapter 10 I quoted at length from an excellent document of the Bishops' Commission on the Liturgical Apostolate, "Reading and Praying in the Vernacular." This text reiterates Miss Brusselman's thought about the need for sincerity in prayer and meaningfulness of gesture. In addition, it contains concrete suggestions for the realization of that ideal in practice.

When the celebrant leads the people in prayer, or speaks to them, or addresses God in their behalf, his manner of speaking will differ somewhat in each case. In every instance, however, he should convey that he sincerely means what he says. This sincerity is crucially important; it makes the difference between a matter-of-fact, ritualized, indifferent celebration and one that is truly an expression of faith and devotion.

1. Dialogue. In the greetings and verbal exchange between celebrant and congregation, all participants should speak their parts with meaning. When the priest says, "The Lord be with you," for example, he must convey that he is really addressing the people, that he sincerely means the

greeting, and that he invites response. The tone and inflection of voice must be natural and convincing. At the same time, dialogue should never become extremely informal; all must be aware that the words they speak are part of a sacred rite. The liturgy must always be characterized by dignity and reverence as well as meaningful and sincere speech.

2. Prayer. When reading the orations, preface, and the like, the priest should speak in a manner befitting his sacerdotal role. His tone of voice should be more formal, more reverent; yet he must remember he is speaking to a Person, not merely reciting formulas. Note that this applies no matter which language is used in the prayer; it applies equally to the Canon as to the collect or the Lord's Prayer. The latter prayer is gravely abused by a sing-song recitation which pays little attention to the praises and petitions actually contained in the words. The conclusions of prayers, although in set formulas, must never be hurried, or routinely said. Since the affirmative response of the people is expected, the rhythm and tone of the priest should be sufficiently strong to encourage and facilitate the response.[3]

The General Instruction of the Roman Missal puts this in terse terms. "The presidential prayers should be spoken in a loud and clear voice so that everyone present can hear and pay attention."[4] It also, however, implies that the celebrant bears a unique responsibility for fostering an interchange between himself and the congregation. He should seek to encourage, to elicit from them a response when he greets them or invites them to pray. "Since the celebration of Mass is a communal action, the dialogue between the celebrant and the congregation and the acclamations are of special value. They constitute the external sign of the communal celebration and are also the means of greater communication between priest and people."[5]

"The Lord be with you," for example, can be a muffled sentence, muttered to one's self with downcast eyes and slightly extended hands. Or, and preferably, it can be a clear greeting, spoken to all with visual expression and welcoming arms. We need not overdo this gesture or force ourselves into unnatural and uncomfortable smiles and gyrations. Nevertheless some life or interest, an awareness of what we are saying and to whom and for what reason gives this short, yet extremely significant phrase the element of sincerity and meaning necessary to evoke a proper response from the lips (and hearts) of a congregation.

The revised Order of Mass facilitates the kind of communication through sight and sound we are discussing. Vatican II Fathers decreed, "In this restoration, both texts and rites should be drawn up so that they express more clearly the holy things which they signify."[6] Most priests, I think, would agree that the present reforms represent a major step in the direction of that goal. The formats for both eucharistic celebrations and other liturgical services seem to possess a nobler simplicity, are shorter, clearer, with fewer useless repetitions, appear more within the people's powers of comprehension, and for the most part do not require much explanation.[7]

Quite simply stated, the alert and concerned celebrant can, with these renewed rites, more easily proclaim a message to his people. The words say something in themselves. Furthermore, simplified and freer rubrical guidelines enable a priest to reinforce or expand the verbal content with bodily gestures and ritualistic actions which are more personal, natural, and thus more sincere and meaningful. It remains for me in this section on communication to suggest certain practical steps as aids for celebrants of the Eucharist in that proclamation process.

The function of the entrance or introductory rites is "to help the assembled people make themselves a worshiping community and to prepare them for listening to God's word and celebrating the eucharist."[8] The celebrant contributes to this "gathering together, building a community process" when he, as we have noted earlier, stands in front of the church and greets his parishioners before Mass. He needs also to wait until the opening hymn or psalm is finished (and the singing should be prolonged sufficiently to achieve its purpose — "to open the celebration, deepen the unity of the people, and introduce them to the mystery of the season or feast. . ."[9]). A brief pause, a swift, silent glance at the congregation, and a clear, reverent, firm sign of the cross which allows and encourages the people to conclude with their "Amen" insures a strong start for the celebration.

The greeting, which "expresses the presence of the Lord in the assembled community,"[10] should be addressed to the persons gathered for worship, not read from the pages of a book (or worse, from the missalette). The priest's extended arms is a welcoming gesture, meant to accompany and state in action what the greeting conveys through words. (Increasingly, celebrants are mastering and memorizing the greetings and other texts for the introductory rites. The obstacle to proper leadership may next be, not an awkward unfamiliarity or slavish dependence on the missal, but the peril of routinely reciting commonplace formulas. I have no easy and pat solution to that problem.)

For the opening prayer which concludes the introductory rites, "the priest invites the people to pray, and together they spend some moments in silence so they may realize that they are in God's presence and may make their petitions."[11] The celebrant, having paused long enough so that he and his community can in fact pray silently, then gathers all these personal, private wishes and presents them in the name of this congregation to the Creator. That collect "expresses the theme of the celebration and is a priestly petition addressed to God the Father through the mediation of Christ in the Holy Spirit. The people make the prayer their own and give their assent by the acclamation, Amen."[12] The earlier quotation from the recommendation of the Bishops' Commission on the Liturgical Apostolate detailed how orations should be prayed. It is for every priest to work out a special, individual style based on those principles. It is for him also to develop personal pauses and gestures that fulfill at this moment a liturgical purpose, not merely to satisfy rubrical laws.

The period for the preparation of bread and wine "is also the appropriate time for the collection of money or gifts for the poor and the Church."[13] An increasing number of parishes have the celebrant sit during this action. Father Hovda, in his *Manual of Celebration*, offers some sound suggestions for taking up the collection:

> Then the president sits in his chair and all are seated, while the ushers gather the money offerings (from the ministers as well as from the rest of the people). It is appropriate — and, we would say, advisable — to announce, at the usual time for

announcements (before the dismissal), the cause or causes outside the community to which the money of this particular offering is going, and the portion of it going to that cause, so that the community is clear that Christian stewardship is not merely church maintenance but is concrete help for the poor and suffering.

The money offering has been treated in many parishes and communities like an embarrassment. It has been taken up while some other liturgical action is going on, and then sneaked off to the sacristy or rectory. The money offering is a part of the liturgy and an extremely important sign. Therefore, all should sit and wait until the ushers have completed the gathering of the offerings before proceeding with the presentation of the gifts.[14]

I agree with Hovda and would add a few additional suggestions. There should be ample and well-trained ushers. We are not allowed today the luxury of foolishly wasted moments in liturgy and an adequate number of well-trained ushers helps avoid that danger. They can see to it that the collection, while done slowly, is still completed swiftly. In addition, baskets passed from person to person rather than longhandled containers pushed rhythmically in and out of each pew by well-meaning, but sometimes abrupt, ushers, increase congregational participation. Furthermore, representatives of the parish (varied each week and selected by the parish worship committee) bearing these gifts to the altar, rather than identical ushers Sunday after Sunday, will add an element of freshness to the celebration.

Finally, Father Hovda's recommendation about the minister's contributing to the collection makes very good sense. For the celebrant communicates when he sits quietly as the ushers move through the church, then accepts the gifts at the altar (with a smile and a word of appreciation), and drops in his own the-night-before-filled envelope. It teaches quietly and explains without a word the meaning of this collection and the function of a priest as leader, sharer, servant in the community.

Since the "offertory" is not really an offering, but a simple preparation of the gifts (the true offering occurs in the memorial following the narrative of the institution), the celebrant and planning committee should not overemphasize this part of the service or insert overdone notions of "offering to God our gifts and our lives." A certain aspect of giving is naturally present, but concentration on it detracts from the fuller, richer, and later memorial offering. There "the Church's intention is for the faithful not only to offer the spotless victim but also to learn to offer themselves and daily to be drawn into ever more perfect union, through Christ the Mediator, with the Father and with each other, so that God may be all things in all."[15] But here we merely prepare gifts. Practically speaking this understanding affects the choice of hymns (not specifically offering ones), the type of gestures (paten and chalice are to be only "slightly raised above the altar,"[16] a showing to the people, not an offering to God), and the tone of voice (words recited quietly, not proclaimed as of major importance).

The retention of offertory prayers, the washing of hands, and the "Orate, fratres" was, in the view of some liturgical experts, unfortunate. Ill-advised or no, we should make the best of them. The congregation will benefit from and appreciate an occasional running explanation of the texts, particularly a word on the Jewish background of the "Blessed are you. . ." prayers. A celebrant who truly and clearly washes his hands (not fingers, and with pitcher, basin, and towel, not in a tiny dish with a delicate piece of linen) and turns to all parts of the community while he says "Pray, brethren. . ." lends meaning to both prayer and action.

In the revised *Ordo Missae*, a rubric before the introductory dialogue preceding the preface states: "The priest begins the eucharistic prayer."[17] The preface, then, is not an isolated, independent entity, but a variable text, woven integrally into the structure of the "canon" or, better, Eucharistic Prayer. A booklet on the new Eucharistic Prayers and prefaces published at the time of their introduction in 1968 by the National Conference of Catholic Bishops explains both the function of the preface and the manner in which it should be said or sung.

> Through instruction and structural changes in the missal,
> we perhaps now finally appreciate that the preface is an essential part of the eucharistic prayer. It is midway between

a prayer and a hymn, but above all contains the notion of thanksgiving and praise. In the variable central portion we glance at one or several aspects of the Mystery of Christ and of God's goodness to men which prompts us to thank him with praise. It thus focuses attention around a particular mystery celebrated on this day or at this season. This praising worship is directed to the Father through Christ and sets the pace for the words of praise and thanksgiving which follow.

The Sanctus actually represents something of an intrusion (it interrupts the flow of ideas), even though the placement of this hymn as a regular feature in eucharistic prayers dates back to the fourth century. The concluding phrases of the preface lead into it logically and the celebrant who understands this can by attitude and tone of voice extend an invitation to join with him in vocally expressing praise of God. Such participation becomes an appropriate share in the eucharistic prayer which is so evidently a service of praising gratitude.[18]

The presidential role of a priest is nowhere more pronounced than in the portions of the Eucharistic Prayer which follow the "Holy, Holy, Holy." (Note that the text of the Sanctus reads "Holy Lord, God of hosts," not "Holy, Lord God of hosts.") He truly proclaims at this central point of the Mass and needs to use all his natural talents for communication to hold the congregation and involve them in the action. When the full text has been printed in the participation aids employed by the community before him, the celebrant's task becomes almost impossible. How many priests have felt utter frustration as they have earnestly worked with voice and eyes and arms in this proclamation, then noted parishoners glued to missalettes or heard 1,000 worshipers turn in unison a page during the institution narrative? We analyzed this difficulty in the last chapter; those thoughts hold equal, even greater force with regard to the Eucharistic Prayer.

In their statement on "The Place of Music in Eucharistic Celebrations" the Bishops' Committee on the Liturgy described the meaning of a Eucharistic Prayer and the priest's proclamation of this text.

The eucharistic prayer is the praise and thanksgiving pronounced over the bread and wine which are to be shared in the communion meal. It is an acknowledgment of the Church's faith and discipleship transforming the gifts to be eaten into the Body which Jesus gave and the Blood which he poured out for the life of the world, so that the sharing of the meal commits the Christian to sharing in the mission of Jesus. As a statement of the universal Church's faith it is proclaimed by the president alone. As a statement of the faith of the local assembly it is affirmed and ratified by all those present through acclamations like the great Amen.

Now that the eucharistic prayer is proclaimed in the vernacular the quality of the celebration will be even more dependent upon the celebrant. From the viewpoint of music it is not so important that he sing—to sing the eucharistic prayer for many celebrants would be to detract from its effectiveness—as that he proclaim the prayer in such a way as to elicit a spirited response from the assembly.[19]

Simple steps can help in this proclamation—looking from time to time at the congregation, waiting until they are settled after the Sanctus before beginning, holding host and cup toward them at the words "Take this, all of you. . . ," pausing and looking around the total community at the words "It will be shed for you. . ." before moving on to "and for all men."[20] An interval for silent recall of living or deceased relatives and loved ones (perhaps with a few phrases of introduction, e.g., "We pause for a moment to mention silently the names of those who are alive and need our prayers") does not, in my opinion, conflict with the general intercessions. The congregation as a unit prays in this prayer of the faithful for the wider, more universal needs of the Church, world, nation, community; the remembrance for the living and the dead, on the other hand, possesses a more intimate, personal, individualized character. It also aids the proclaiming process to elevate the cup and paten at sufficient height during the doxology, pivot with them in a semicircle toward the entire congregation, hold both at the suitable level until *after* the "Amen" has been completed, even if this acclamation, repeated several times folk style, takes several moments.

The celebrant who understands the nature of a Eucharistic Prayer, who recognizes his own serious responsibility to preside over the Eucharist and proclaim it with meaning will in time develop a personal style comfortable for him and clear to his people. He should also come to realize that unison, congregational recitation of the Eucharistic Prayer is liturgically unsound, only superficially a step forward toward full participation, and an abdication of his presidential role. The priest has his part to fulfill; the community, theirs. If he performs his duties well, they will be inspired to respond accordingly at the proper occasions.

"*The rite of peace*: before they share in the same bread the people express their love for one another and beg for peace and unity in the Church and with all mankind."[21] This gesture of love and peace has engendered a considerable amount of hostility and turmoil in parishes across the United Sates. Some find it artificial, unhygienic, forced, disrespectful, or irreverent. In a summer, 1969, survey of diocesan liturgical commissions, most liturgy officials marked "poorly" or "indifferently" the reception given to this innovation of the restored liturgy, even though they registered "very well" or "well" on the acceptance tendered other current reforms like the Order of Mass, Lectionary, marriage, and baptismal rites.

We will not here delve into the reasons pro and con for the kiss of peace, but only remark that the celebrant's own attitude can do much either to intensify parishoners' objections or diminish people's resentment. One can legitimately question the suitability of this sign for an American congregation (rubrics speak of the gesture not in terms of a command, but as a suggestion: "Then the deacon (or the priest) may add: 'Let us offer each other the sign of peace.' " The Latin original reads: "*Deinde, pro opportunitate, diaconus, vel sacerdos, subiungit*: '*Offerte vobis pacem*.' ").[22] However, without thorough instruction beforehand, persuasive, gentle encouragement from the pulpit, and positive example at the altar, the gesture of love and reconciliation surely will fail in a church of any size. Heavy-handed edicts from the sanctuary can never bring this off successfully; skillful, patient, relaxed, humor-filled ones may. Time will tell.

"*The breaking of bread*: this gesture of Christ at the Last

Supper gave the entire eucharistic action its name in apostolic times. In addition to its practical aspect, it signifies that in communion we who are many are made one body in the one bread which is Christ (1 Cor. 10:17)."[23] It remains to be seen how long before or if we commonly employ a large, full host which "appears as actual food" and is "made in such a way that the priest can break it and distribute the parts to at least some of the faithful."[24] The women of Father James Shaughnessy's parish in Creve Coeur, Illinois, bake fairly thick, soft, easily broken altar breads which divide into several dozen particles. The priests employ these on both Sundays and weekdays, although for Sabbath celebrations and for special Masses with large crowds, these are supplemented by the small, common commercial or convent-made whole wheat hosts.

A priest can underscore the symbolism of this "fractio panis" by careful, visible actions. The commingling of particle with Precious Blood may be a hidden, unknown ceremony or an open, intelligible one; the division of the larger host at the Lamb of God may be a strange, mysterious action or a clear, understood one; the "This is the Lamb of God" gesture may be the showing of a broken piece of Divine Bread or the holding of a carefully refitted circular host with one tiny fragment missing. Occasional brief explanations of these rites inserted by the celebrant at the proper moment (recommended centuries ago by the Council of Trent) will both deepen parishioners' understanding and remind them of fuller truths they may have forgotten.

Clarke, without discussing the theology of vestments or their value for contemporary man, maintains that from a pragmatic viewpoint they can greatly assist the celebrant in his efforts to make strong and viable gestures.

> If a priest were to stand at the altar in, say, his everyday suit, he would be extremely difficult to pick out from his background. Even if he were to wear a suit which is not black, the problems would remain. He is inevitably at some height and distance from his congregation, and for them to pick out, and concentrate on, any gesture that he might make in that situation would be very difficult.

Put the same man into a chasuble and the situation is completely changed. Immediately his size is increased. Any gesture that he may make must be larger and therefore much clearer. This makes the Mass easier to follow, with the result that the congregational responses become much stronger and the rapport between priest and people far better.[25]

The pre-Vatican II Mass found a celebrant making some fifty signs of the cross — upon himself, over the gifts, toward the people. The simpler restored Order of Mass calls for three (four with the Roman canon) only, at the beginning and end of the celebration and at the consecratory epiclesis when "the Church calls on God's power and asks that the gifts offered by men may become the body and blood of Christ."[26] The concluding benediction, it seems to me, should be executed with a sense of splendor and solemnity. Not, of course, in an overly dramatic way, but with precision and expansiveness of movement which truly proclaims that the leader of worship is asking the almighty Father and Blessed Trinity to bless members of this community before he sends them out "in peace to love and serve the Lord."[27]

Chapter 13

PLANNING THE LITURGY

In our seminary days the pastoral theology professor cautioned us about the poor habits of some priests who rush from bed sheets to altar linens. He was warning, of course, about the lack of proper preparation on a celebrant's part for the sacred mysteries. However, the instructor meant at that time only to stress the need for private prayer and personal meditation as a prelude to the daily exercise of one's priestly ministry. His words contained few or no references to planning the Mass, to selecting the most suitable texts, to establishing a theme for the service.

We had few options then. For example, the nuptial Mass provided a single epistle and gospel, a standard blessing, one set of prayers. Priests knew only the Roman canon and a complicated *ordo* specified exactly what texts were proper for each day of the year. Seldom was there a choice, although requiem Masses were permitted on most occasions. The rites for baptisms and funerals followed identical patterns whether for infant or adult, for the tragic death of a teen-ager or the long-expected demise of an octogenarian. The Roman liturgy was, in a word, inflexible.

No longer. Flexibility is, as we have frequently observed, the central characteristic of our revised liturgical books. Official documents talk in terms of adaptability—by the national conference of bishops to the needs of a nation, by the local ordinary to the traditions of a diocese, by the individual celebrant to the circumstances of a worshiping community.

Such flexibility and adaptability means a choice and demands decision-making. For intelligent and productive choices or decisions, the leader of worship must plan a liturgy, select the best options, and consider the specific conditions of the congregation over which he is to preside.[1]

The General Instruction insists from the very beginning on the necessity of this planning and preparation for optimum use of the reformed rites:

> This purpose will be accomplished if the celebration takes into account the nature and circumstances of each assembly and is planned to bring about conscious, active, and full participation of the people, motivated by faith, hope and charity.
>
> The celebration of the eucharist and the entire liturgy is carried out by use of signs. By these signs faith is nourished, strengthened, and expressed. It is thus very important to select and arrange the forms and elements proposed by the Church, which, taking into account individual and local circumstances, will best foster active and full participation and promote the spiritual welfare of the faithful.[2]

"All concerned should work together in preparing the ceremonies, pastoral arrangements, and music for each celebration. They should work under the direction of the rector and should consult the people about the parts which belong to them."[3] These short directives prove not so simple in practice.

To sit down with an enthusiastic young couple and describe the options available to them for their approaching marriage ceremony is relatively easy. We will suggest in the second section of this book some practical measures which can aid the celebrant in this particular task. The process becomes a bit more complicated with baptism since we often have several infants (and sets of parents) involved. Planning the details of a funeral rite with the bereaved may also run into difficulties due to the shortness of time on hand for such preparations and the emotional condition of a family.

Careful preparation for the Sunday schedule of Masses, however, makes the shared decision-making for weddings, baptisms, or funerals seem, in comparison, incredibly facile. How do you evaluate the worship needs of a large, heterogeneous community and translate that into an arrangement satisfactory for all or even the majority? Priests who have sampled a parish in an effort merely to determine the desirable hours for weekly services almost throw their hands up in despair at the conflicting responses. If we have trouble reaching a consensus on such a mechanical matter, then what about the task of sifting out preferences in deeper, more personal concerns (organ or guitar music? recited or sung responses? kiss of peace? offertory procession?). It appears enormously complicated, time-consuming, full of frustrations. And it is. Yet any liturgical program will surely fail without some type of serious, relatively scientific, and informed advance planning.

Preparing the liturgy for a small worshiping community obviously is much easier and will be more successful than planning services for a large one. To celebrate a home Mass for ten couples may require only a lengthy telephone conversation with the individual delegated to handle that responsibility or an hour with the several persons designated to plan this Eucharist. Very likely, too, these efforts may seem highly productive with the actual liturgy moving the participants and fulfilling their needs. To organize a varied, flexible, high-quality program for six Sunday Masses and several thousand people is a totally different project. It demands a wider planning committee, definite structures, longer hours, and produces, in many ways, far less rewarding results. Part II includes a chapter on the organization, purpose, and functional operation of such parish worship commissions. Here I wish only to touch on certain characteristics of the planned liturgy which a priest should strive for as he works alone and with others in preparing the celebration.

The liturgy ought to be *flexible*. This flexibility refers to the texts and ceremonial options, to the resources available in a community for worship, and to the temperament of the members in a specific congregation.

First of all, those planning a liturgical celebration need to explore all the alternative texts provided and investigate possible variations in the ceremony itself. The marriage service is, perhaps, the clearest illustration. Its twenty-eight readings and numerous prayers or blessings should be considered beforehand, ideally by the couple contemplating matrimony; the different ceremonial possibilities, e.g., parental involvement in the processional march, members of the wedding party as lectors, likewise ought to be discussed.

Other celebrations — baptisms, funerals, Sunday and weekday Masses — may not lend themselves so easily to shared preparation of texts and ceremonies by priest and community, but the fundamental pattern can be observed. In doing so, the planning committee should follow these principles established in the General Instruction.

> The pastoral effectiveness of a celebration depends in great measure on choosing readings, prayers, and songs which correspond to the needs, spiritual preparation, and attitude of the participants. This will be achieved by an intelligent use of the options which are described below.
>
> In planning the celebration, the priest should consider the spiritual good of the assembly rather than his own desires. The choice of texts is to be made in consultation with the ministers and others who have a function in the celebration, including the faithful.
>
> Since a variety of options is provided, it is necessary for the deacon, readers, cantors, commentator, and choir to know beforehand the texts for which they are responsible, so that nothing will upset the celebration. This careful planning will help dispose the people to take their part in the eucharist.[4]

The texts of a liturgy go beyond official readings, prayers, and processional changes. They include hymns, a prayer of the faithful, comments before each scriptural excerpt, introductory and

concluding remarks, the homily, and any other incidental explanations which will better "dispose the people to take their part
in the eucharist." These entail composition as well as selection
and presuppose some central theme or themes which can unify
the total worship service.

A flexible liturgy will also take full advantage of the resources
(lectors, musicians, ushers, etc.) residing in a community.
Hence, the programs for Sundays in rural parishes usually
adhere to simple patterns since, in those small villages, good
organists are quite rare, competent lectors often hard to develop,
and other instrumentalists seldom available. This does not, of
course, preclude the possibility of excellent liturgical celebrations. On the contrary, country churches, tiny in size and few in
number, with members of the congregation well-known to each
other and to the pastor, present almost unexcelled opportunities
for warm, personal, worship services.

Celebrants in mammoth urban and suburban units, on the
other hand, encounter nearly insuperable liturgical obstacles—impersonalism caused by a huge and transient type of
membership, poor acoustics and visibility in the building itself,
extensive and factory-like schedules. Yet parish planning committees work here with compensating benefits—an abundance of
personnel, the possibility of arranging different Masses for
varied temperaments, ample budgetary resources for participation aids and professional assistance. "Folk" Eucharists, for example, with guitar, flute, and bass violin, occur regularly in certain city parishes and the churches of suburbia; the celebrant
with such talent in a rural community would be uniquely blessed
and highly fortunate.

The priest's role and the function of a worship commission is
to uncover these talented persons in a parish and then use them
fully in the liturgy.

Flexibility, finally, entails a sensitive evaluation of liturgical
attitudes in the total community and a preparation of services
satisfactory, and thus fruitful, for the greatest number. Priests already understand well and newly formed parish liturgy committees will soon learn that this task is hazardous and full of disap-
pointments. One never pleases all, and always alienates some.

The well-meaning, middle-of-the-road, reconciling speaker, writer, or liturgy planner runs into flak from both sides. He runs too fast and too far for those who wish to drag along; he waits too long and walks too slowly for those who seek to dash ahead.

I experienced these reactions when my column "Worship and the World" began to appear in diocesan newspapers. The articles were, I thought, mild, balanced, and, of course divinely inspired. They surely would be acceptable to progressives and traditionalists alike. In this age of polarization, I dreamily conjectured, this writer would become the healing savior. In one carefully written piece on penance I particularly expected to please all those of conservative bent by defending the great merits of auricular confession, those of a change mentality by recommending rather strongly certain modifications in confessional procedures. The letter which follows reveals how well I succeeded.

> Your article entitled "Bless Me Father" is a piece of rubbish of which you should be ashamed.
>
> I have clipped and am enclosing the third paragraph of your article to emphasize my objections. What kind of puerile, retarded boobies do you think "many people" are that they should need space, ventilation, light, heat, and complete physical comfort while confessing their sins?
>
> I am eighty years old and have been receiving the sacrament of penance regularly since childhood and have been in all kinds of "boxes" — some with curtains, some with doors, etc., and have never yet found one frightening, dark or cramped. And I have never found it difficult to sense that I am meeting Jesus and hearing words of absolution — no matter what kind of person is speaking to me from the other side of the screen. I don't care what color his skin is, whether or not he has red hair or black, or is bald; has a long or short nose; whether he is a priest who likes to talk or not — the ONLY thing that matters is that he is a priest who has the power to forgive sins. And if you think people are going to confession more often when they can sit "face to face" with the confessor you are deluding yourself. . . .
>
> I am devoting the remainder of my life to constant prayer for priests and religious men and women that they may

have the special grace to be faithful to their vows. I am ad-
ding your name henceforth.

Her assurance of prayers pleased me and I am grateful for
them, but the letter raised severe doubts about my ability to reconcile divergent camps. The leader of worship and his planning
committee unquestionably will feel similar critical jabs from left
and right, young and old, regardless of how thoroughly they
prepare a versatile program designed to match the diversity of
temperaments in their community.

The pastor of St. Anthony's Parish in Washington, D.C., tried
to cope with this problem through a varied Sunday Mass schedule published in the bulletin and listed in the large announcement
box outside the church.

6:00 7:00 8:15 LOW
9:30 10:45 SINGING
12:00 FOLK
1:15 P.M. LATIN 6:00 P.M. LOW

He arrived at this program through a survey in which
parishioners indicated their choices for the times of Masses and
the kinds of celebrations. A year or so later the Latin service
was dropped apparently because of decreasing interest and at-
tendance.

Such a flexible, well-publicized schedule based on careful
research of the community's desires certainly represents a step
in the right direction. However, frequently repeated soundings
of the congregation should also be made to evaluate other components of Sunday services as well: the homilies, the musical
programs, the performance of lectors. That again calls for well-
organized, hard-working, and competently staffed parish worship committees. In this way, "If he celebrates with a congregation," the priest can "first consider the spiritual good of the
faithful and avoid imposing his own spiritual tastes."[5]

The liturgy ought to be *varied*. America is a land of the free,
and of fads and fashions. We become very excited about a new
food or style of dress or form of recreation, work it to death,

grow weary of the once novel now commonplace, and then turn aside from this to something fresh. It makes and breaks daring entrepreneurs.

Television constantly reflects, perhaps even has caused, this great thirst for variety, change, newness. "Laugh-in" moves rapidly from scene to scene; if you miss one line, have no fear, another crack will come along in a matter of seconds. I found funny at first the sequence in which this program's "dirty old man" hobbles to a park bench, cuddles next to an elderly lady, makes a pass, and is then promptly whacked by the irate and proper female. Six weeks later, however, the generally similar, although slightly altered, interchange had, for me, lost both its punch and its humor.

Fall Sunday afternoons are, we know, for probably a majority of citizens in the United States consecrated to four or five hours of uninterrupted television viewing—in color, if you are lucky; accompanied by beer, if you like it; roars, if your team scores; groans, if your man fumbles. Most husbands love those football games; some wives hate them. They detest the hold these fast-moving, ever-changing, always surprising contests exert upon their spouses. *Nothing* must interfere with their father's Sabbath pleasure, children are told, even if the doubleheader begins at 1:00 P.M. and ends in the early evening.

The liturgy must willy-nilly compete with such television. This does not mean we should return to the days in which worship was a silent, spectator event. Nor ought we so jazz up the service that parishioners become uncomfortable, alienated, and unable to recognize the fundamental structure of a Eucharist. But we must inject a certain element of freshness and variety into the weekly worship service.

Parishioners understandably tire of the same four hymns repeated month after month after month. One can ask if we have not reached a point of liturgical sophistication in which Catholics find the weekly "hymn at entrance, offertory, Communion and recession" pattern wearisome and generally uninspiring. More and more alert parishes attempt to vary at least slightly their program for a given Sunday Mass. For example, on one Sunday the congregation at the presentation of gifts sings a hymn; on the next, the choir or folk group harmonizes on their own; on the next, instrumentalists perform a background piece of music; on the next, a cantor leads the community in antiphonal psalm singing; on the next, the congregation silently, attentively observes the celebrant as he prepares bread and wine.

Extremes should be avoided in providing a varied type of liturgy. Parishioners will neither sing nor respond well unless they feel secure and at ease. No one enjoys acting like a fool. Better be a silent worshiper than to stand out as an off-key, "Don't you know the melody!" participant. Thus any variations should be introduced gradually, with adequate explanation and rehearsal, and clearly, so each person knows exactly where to find the text, when to join in, and what to say or sing. Too many, too complicated changes made too swiftly will never be accepted by a congregation.

The opposite course — a rigid, standard sameness — dulls Sunday Mass and diminishes the faithful's full appreciation of the sacred mysteries. The Mass is the Mass, naturally, "but in order that the sacred liturgy may produce its full effect, it is necessary that the faithful come to it with proper dispositions, that their thoughts match their words, and that they cooperate with divine grace lest they receive it in vain."[6] Celebrants, to illustrate, who employ only Eucharistic Prayer II (because it is the shortest) or III (because it is especially suited for Sunday) fail to take advantage of the options in the official liturgical books and impoverish, spiritually, those for whom they are responsible.

When parishioners comment that the Sunday celebration seems varied but comfortable, fresh but familiar; when they praise the variety, yet still feel secure — the planners of worship in that community have done well.

The liturgy ought to be of the highest possible *quality*.

It is wonderful to have a conscientious "folk group" for Sunday Mass, but if they noisily drop their guitars and bass violin during the Eucharistic Prayer, if they insist on two dozen verses of their favorite hymn, if they fool around in front of the congregation, then this combo becomes a liability. It is marvelous to see an entire community march to the altar for Communion, but when priests of the parish mix up their signals and fail to show in sufficient number for the distribution of the Eucharist, the liturgy suffers. It is gratifying to have volunteer organists serve with great regularity; but if they play the hymns at an unsingable pace or key, participation soon stops. It is a blessing to have a large, talented choir, but if they misunderstand their function and dominate the scene, then we don't really have quality liturgy.

Quality liturgy occurs, very simply, when each person with a special function to fulfill does it well. The Council Fathers made the point in these words:

> Servers, lectors, commentators, and members of the choir also exercise a genuine liturgical ministry. They ought, therefore, to discharge their office with a sincere piety and decorum demanded by so exalted a ministry and rightly expected of them by God's people.
>
> Consequently they must all be deeply penetrated with the spirit of the liturgy, each in his own measure, and they must be trained to perform their functions in a correct and orderly manner.[7]

In addition to those named specifically these phrases include and, more, refer especially to the celebrant; they exclude, however, in my judgment, the congregation. We encourage the community to sing, to respond, to participate fully and well, and are delighted when they do so. But I would prefer people to sing poorly, than not to sing at all, to respond incorrectly, than not to respond at all, to join in at the wrong moments, than not to join at all. To scold parishioners, for example, about their poor performance or rebuke them for their lack of musical talent is out of order and sabotages worship in the name of artistic or aesthetic perfection.

Instead, we try to arrange quality liturgies, making the best of the resources (limited though they may be) that exist in the community. We carefully train the servers, lectors, and commentators. We guide the choir in its rehearsals. We plan, with the help of others where feasible, a flexible and varied worship program. We work at our own role as a celebrant, as a leader of prayer, as a president of the community. Then we leave the rest to God and to his people.

Sometimes, sometimes, it comes off. Sometimes we can almost feel the power of a quality eucharistic celebration as it "draws the faithful into a compelling love of Christ and sets them afire."[8] We can't predict those occasions. The weather, the mood of a nation, the spirit of a parish, the celebrant's charism, the choir's enthusiasm, the texts of that Sunday or feast—these must curiously mesh with countless other unpredictable and imperceptible factors. But when they do (one cannot expect this each Sunday, nor regularly, nor even frequently), we know it, we experience a deeply spiritual, a profound and unforgettable religious event. Those moments sustain us through more ordinary, routine eucharistic services, just as times of joy and elation in life carry us through periods of sorrow and worry or through the drab, everyday routine of ordinary living.

Yet even during those common, those almost disappointing worship services, "grace is channeled into us." We receive it "from the liturgy, therefore, and especially from the Eucharist, as from a fountain."[9] We may not sense this; in fact no one may feel it at a given celebration (the workings of God in the hearts of man can be hidden temporarily from all, particularly the person most affected). But the reality is there. Men are being sanctified in Christ, God is being glorified.[10] Here "God in Christ sanctifies the world and men adore the Father through Christ, his Son."[11]

This is the role of a priest in the flexible liturgy: to lead men in worship, above all through the celebration of Mass, that action of Christ and of God's people which stands at the center of our Christian life.[12]

PART II

WORSHIP AT THE MAJOR MOMENTS IN LIFE

Chapter 1

THE PARISH
WORSHIP COMMITTEE

Men are easily moved at the major moments of life. A baby's birth brings joy, pride, and protectiveness into the hearts of parents. Failure (moral or otherwise) forces a person to look deeply into his heart and make some radical decisions about the direction in which he will turn tomorrow. Couples promise nervously, seriously, and happily at their wedding to live and love together as husband and wife until death. The approach of life's end sobers even a most flippant individual, while final separation of a loved one from our midst leaves heavy hearts and drained emotions, a present aching emptiness and hopeful expectations for eternal life in the future.

Because these events are charged with feeling, the liturgical rites with which we surround them can readily touch participants. They feel joy, remorse, love, sorrow. If the worship service somehow expresses those inner feelings, if the liturgy speaks about this significant event and sheds some light on its meaning, if it captures the spirit of the community assembled for prayer, then people will walk away pleased, enlightened, and inspired. In this section of the book, I will discuss baptism, reconciliation or penance, marriage, death and dying. The different chapters will offer some background theological material and practical pastoral suggestions for liturgical celebrations in each of these cases. As I indicated in the Introduction, these pages in no way pretend to cover exhaustively all the possibilities nor should the volume be judged as a complete manual for celebrants or parish worship committees. Perhaps, however, both may find its ideas and recommendations helpful in planning the liturgy for these important occasions in the lives of men.

Sunday services present a more complex situation. Parishioners usually arrive at church in various moods and with different concerns running through their minds. Since our reactions to external forces—the music, the texts, the homily—tend to be highly subjective and colored, as I mentioned in the earlier chapter on preaching, by what preoccupies us at this instant, each worshiper responds in a unique way to every celebration. One can quickly discover this by quizzing a few honest persons after Mass. Their positive or negative comments about the sermon generally emanate from a basic predisposition within them. They came with an anxiety and you accidentally happened to air it; they felt confused about some development inside or outside the Church and you intentionally or otherwise clarified it; they possess strong convictions on a subject and you spoke of it.

There are occasions, however, when circumstances on the global, national, or local level create a unified climate in a worshiping community. The death of John F. Kennedy, cited in a previous section, perhaps represents one classic illustration, the first moon landing another, the return of a malfunctioning space ship with possibly doomed occupants, a third. A Sunday liturgy which reflected the thoughts and feelings of Americans at those moments would truly hold their attention and involve them in the service. Today's Mass, they would say, was real, relevant, down-to-earth, practical, fantastic. On other days the celebration might in fact have been technically better, more carefully planned and properly executed, but the congregation could not, psychologically, react as sensitively as they did during those hours of crisis.

Local situations of deep common interest can cause a similar phenomenon. Prospects of a black or brown influx into an isolated all-white suburb; the tragic death of a young, well-known, and deeply loved parishioner; the Easter outpouring of happy families in bright colors with beautiful corsages on a gorgeous spring day—events like these and the powerful emotions unleashed by them bind a congregation together. They charge the atmosphere, unite people, and open worshipers to a message which somehow relates to their jointly experienced feelings.

One must possess extremely sensitive, ever active antennae to catch the prevailing mood of a parish. And, as must be evident from our discussion, there is not always and every Sunday a dominant character or tone in the congregation. The celebrant and his worship committee embarks, therefore, on an intricate, delicate mission. They should evaluate the general and individual needs of parishioners and prepare Sunday and special celebrations which reflect those constantly shifting concerns.

A. Organization

In our outlining steps for establishing a parish or community worship committee we should always keep in mind that structures are not ends in themselves, but only means to reach a goal. The leader of a congregation must first determine the size and type of his community, then decide just what kind of organizational setup would work most effectively in this situation. Small, rural units neither require involved committees nor generally possess the personnel to staff such planning groups. Large city and suburban complexes, however, demand more elaborate structures, tighter rules of procedure, and more extensive and representative membership. In any event, I offer the suggestions which follow with the understood reservation that each parish or community ultimately will adapt these norms to their peculiar circumstances.

We have at the time of this writing no national booklet available as a reference manual for the development of liturgy planning committees. Father Hovda's *Manual of Celebration* contains a few useful pages on the subject which could stimulate thinking and serve as generalized guidelines.[1] Several diocesan liturgical commissions, in addition, have published pamphlets on the parish liturgy team.[2] These are valuable, but were not intended for mass distribution, often treat of specialized, local questions, and frequently overlap. The last characteristic is due to the praiseworthy "holy thievery" which, we happily admit, has been happening in the past year or so among commissions in the United States. The remarks below mix material from these sources and ideas gleaned from my personal observations.

The fundamental, essential principle in selecting or electing members is "across the board" representation. To the extent feasible, every segment of the community plus delegates from those groups immediately engaged in liturgical preparation (musicians, lectors, ushers) should be included on the committee. This means, first of all and naturally, the celebrants. In parishes with several priests on the staff it is especially imperative that all of them attend the meetings, or at least hear accurate accounts of the proceedings, contribute their opinions, and follow the procedures agreed upon. If celebrants poorly communicate with each other in a rectory, then they cannot expect to communicate well with parishioners in a church. The absence of cohesive planning by priests and worship committee or, worse, disregard for the efforts of the liturgy commission by one, some, or all of the celebrants scuttles the structure before it gets off the ground.

Next, on the worship unit, come delegates of those so-called performers in the actual liturgy itself. The organist, choir director, folk combo leader, head of the cantors, chairman of the lectors, and president of the ushers — all should be present. A full-time, competently trained, properly paid parish music director would greatly simplify this procedure and surely enhance the quality of liturgical celebrations in a parish. In fact, I grow daily more convinced that until we truly commit ourselves to adequate musical budgets—for professional personnel and printed texts (not mimeographed sheets of copyright material)—parish worship will never reach the level desired nor fulfill the functions projected by Vatican II.

We need also a representative of the religious in the community, and resource persons of special talents who may be available. The latter might mean an artist, architect, writer, scholar, dramatist, school administrator, CCD teacher, or in fact anyone with a unique background that could render service in the preparation of liturgies.

Finally, some method of hearing what different facets of the congregation have to say ought to be devised. We should listen to senior citizens, married persons, young people, women, single individuals and determine what are their wishes with regard to worship. The parish liturgical committee of Blessed Sacrament Parish in Alexandria, Virginia, for example, has a membership of nearly twenty including a bearded teen-ager and a mother of several children. The commission, then, should be filled out with enough random delegates to catch some of the attitudes from major blocs of parishioners.

How choose these members? The elective process strikes us immediately as ideal, but I wonder if in the beginning this might not turn into something of a disaster. Instead, in my judgment, at the start the priest ought to appoint an adequate number of talented persons who will form a both competent and truly representative body. (Obviously he should be intelligent and secure enough to avoid naming "yes men" for the committee or filling it with uninterested people.) Once the new commission is in operation, a program of liturgical catechesis in the community could be planned which will inform parishioners about the nature and purpose of the worship committee. Simultaneously, a subcommittee might design tentative plans for future elections which would include definite, staggered terms of office.

The insistence on precise, rotation tours of duty is crucial for the success of the parish worship committee. It insures a constant influx of fresh faces and imaginative minds, yet protects the group's stability and assures a continuity in its work. This clear delineation likewise enables the committee to cleanse itself of deadwood without offending those less productive members. Finally, men tend to work harder and better, and feel happier, when they accept responsibility for a specific task which will be completed within determined time limits.

The method of conducting regular meetings will depend upon the worship committee's size. It would be preferable to have someone other than the pastor or parish priest serve as chairman and, if the group warrants it, an executive body to plan in advance the agenda and tentatively determine overall policy. These points, however, are largely incidental. What does matter is the efficient arrangement of officers, subcommittees, agenda, and procedures so that general sessions run smoothly, democratically, and productively.

Meetings may indeed be modern man's cross, but long, wandering, inconclusive discussions indicate either the absence of a competent chairman or the existence of an unworkable system. The leader, for instance, who allows debate on any point, minor or major, to occupy an excessive amount of time at a plenary gathering has failed in his role. He should recognize either a consensus about to materialize or the need for referral to a subcommittee. General sessions need to face problems, air views, make decisions, and then move on. The chairman's function demands astute judgment and delicate tact. Participants must not feel their voice is unheard, but neither should they return home groaning with frustration over a poorly chaired, aimless evening of talk which produced no conclusion—except the resolution to convene again. Busy, important people with the talents and background so desirable for a committee of this importance in the parish will be more disposed to lend valuable moments if they know the committee operates effectively and won't waste their time.

To achieve that goal two particular elements are indispensable: a liberal use of both on-going and ad hoc subcommittees and some clear delegation of authority by the pastor or celebrant to the worship committee itself. The former keeps plenary sessions on target and permits detailed examination of specific points by a smaller cluster of individuals. When subcommittees operate properly, the full membership can concentrate on wide issues and long-range plans without bogging down in minutiae. The latter point — clear, delegated authority — instills confidence and begets a sense of responsibility in the committee. Unless the person who heads the parish or worshiping community seriously considers the decisions of the liturgy commission, its members will soon grow discouraged, give up, and direct time and energy toward more receptive fields. Here money talks louder than words. When a pastor allocates an adequate budget for the liturgy and worship committee, he tells members by his actions that he trusts them, hopes they work at the task, and will respect their judgments whenever feasible. In short, he bestows authority upon the commission through a grant of working funds (minimal though these may be, relatively speaking) for its operation.

B. Goals and Purposes

The goals and purposes of a parish worship committee could be categorized under five headings: self-education, spiritual self-growth, parish education, community evaluation, and liturgy preparation.

Self-education. A sizable worship committee or one which satisfactorily represents the various segments of a community does not automatically succeed and function correctly. The members must possess at least a rudimentary understanding of and appreciation for the liturgy. They should have sound notions of what is good worship and how this type of liturgical celebration is achieved. Education of the entire group and of each member, therefore, is the virtual launching point in any development of a worship commission.

Several practical measures come to mind in this context. Part of every session should be dedicated to education in the liturgy.

This might mean a speaker, a paper, a book report, a tape, a filmstrip. The educational portion need not, indeed ought not, to run on for any great length (ten or fifteen minutes would seem adequate). Fidelity to some program of this type, however, gradually will deepen the member's insights and sharpen their abilities to make good decisions.

Providing each person with catechetical materials on the liturgy is an obvious tool in the educational process. Individual or bulk subscriptions to current periodicals (*Worship*, *Parish Today*, publications from the Liturgical Conference, *Newsletter* from the Bishops' Committee on the Liturgy, materials from a diocesan liturgical commission) would be helpful. So, too, a lending library of books. The Chicago booklet, *Parish Liturgy Team*, offers a bibliography which could prove useful as a guide in this at the outset.[3]

Finally, nothing can compare in value to a personal exchange with officers or members of other parish or community worship committees. The 1970 National Meeting of Diocesan Liturgical Commissions dedicated an afternoon workshop to this subject of Parish Worship Committees. A member sent there by the committee (this is where the budget becomes imperative) would have gathered a quantity of printed items, caught a few fresh ideas, and met at meals or between sessions many individuals eager to share experiences. National or regional conferences of this nature may not always be available, but an interchange on the local level requires little effort and less expense, only some initiative.

Spiritual self-growth. The worship committee which fails to perceive that the liturgy is prayer, pure and simple, may find itself "a gong booming or a cymbal clashing."[4] Communal prayer to the Father through Christ around the table of the Word and of the Lord *is* the Church at its fullest and finest. Christ is present in this worship, but he also really dwells among us when we gather for prayer or listen to his word in the Bible.[5]

It follows that every meeting should begin with some form of prayer (informally composed on an alternating basis by different participants can be powerful) and include a brief reflective reading of sacred scripture. An occasional Mass for the entire group is almost to be expected. These spiritual "exercises" ought to promote growth in the hearts of every member and remind all that their task is a noble one.

Parish education. The introduction of revised official liturgical books from Rome and the implementation of decisions by the National Conference of Catholic Bishops in the United States require a catechesis for the laity. Up to this point the burden generally rested upon the shoulders of parish priests and the Sunday sermon or parish bulletin served as the main vehicle of information. We can hope that soon active, well-organized worship committees may assume most of the responsibility. The educational process must go on for we will need both to inform the faithful about future changes in the liturgy and to improve their grasp of the rites we now follow.

To accomplish this the worship committee could sponsor lectures, workshops, liturgical weekends; arrange home study programs; organize a series of small group Eucharists; develop a community lending liturgical library; write a weekly section for the parish bulletin; initiate a newsletter mailed directly to parishioners. The last suggestion would be easy for a committee of the Paterson Diocese. Its diocesan commission has prepared a monthly circular for purchase in bulk quantities and distribution at the church door or through regular mailings.

This educational endeavor should, above all, seek to inform parishioners about the activities of the worship committee: who the members are, when they meet, what decisions they have made, how they can be contacted. Clear channels of communication will convey such information from the liturgy commission to worshipers; it will also conduct feedback from parishioners to the committee members.

Community evaluation. We mentioned in the final chapter of the first section that good liturgy should be flexible. The full textual and ceremonial options ought to be investigated, all resources in a community tapped, and the diversified temperaments of worshipers and parishioners gauged. Such flexibility, especially in terms of resources and attitudes in essence means

an evaluation of the parish or community. The worship committee needs to fashion some thorough methods for discovering
capable musicians, readers, etc., who are willing to serve in the
liturgy and some relatively accurate procedures for measuring
the preferences of worshipers. With this type of data in its pos-
session, the liturgical commission can then attempt to construct
a new schedule of services or revise an old one.

Father Robert M. Peet, pastor of St. Roch's Parish in St.
Louis, has organized and normally follows the advice of his
parish council on these things. Split sociologically three ways — a
predominantly white, upper middle class sector, a black-white
middle income section, a mostly black slum area — this territorial
church is also divided, after the pattern of most American
parishes, into conservative, progressive, and in-between fac-
tions. The pastor and parish council have, over the past few
years, experimented more or less successfully with different
Sunday schedules in an effort to satisfy this highly complex mix-
ture of individuals. They tried an innovative Eucharist in the
school, transferred it to the church as the last Sunday Mass after
objections had been raised, then moved the more modern service back to the school, but on Saturday afternoon. The present
Sunday program is typical of a large parish in the United States
with quiet, hymn, choir, and contemporary Masses interspersed
throughout the day. Not all members of St. Roch's feel content
with the situation, but the vast majority know a realistic attempt
has been made to tackle these problems and appreciate the fact
that their objections have been registered and their opinions
weighed.[6]

The uneven results and frequently altered schedule at St.
Roch's underscores the necessity for regular evaluation by the
parish worship committee of current programs. How well do the
people like this new change or that innovation? What suggestions do they wish to offer? Are the homilies and the parish
bulletin inserts beneficial and satisfactory, or inadequate? To do
an evaluation the commission might employ questionnaires at
Sunday Mass, spot checking of parishioners by telephone or letter, personal visits to homes, or publicly announced "hearings"

in various regions of the parish. Occasionally printing the names, addresses, and telephone numbers of committee members and inviting parishioners to submit recommendations or criticisms would be a good initial move. Steps like these accomplish a twofold purpose. They offer everyone in the community an opportunity to ventilate hostilities, something very valuable of itself, and they present the commission with an occasion to explain the background behind certain decisions and thus contribute to the liturgical education of each inquirer.

Community evaluation of the liturgy forms part of an overall effort to foster worship of the highest quality. The committee should sample the sentiments of parishioners and select the most attractive options, true, but it also must constantly cast a critical eye toward the "performance" of those who occupy any type of leadership role in the liturgy. How well do the lectors read? Does the organist play too fast, too slow, too high, too low, too loud, too soft, too little, too much? Is the choir dominating the celebration? Has the folk group become a distraction by its appearance or behavior or repertoire? What about the celebrant and his function? The list obviously could go on.

The diocesan liturgical commission in Sacramento, California, with the assistance of some professional speech consultants, prepared this "Criteria for Commentators and Readers." It illustrates the type of evaluative tool an imaginative parish worship committee might use or even create.

CRITERA FOR COMMENTATORS AND READERS

The purpose of an oral reading of a text is to make the text clearly understandable to someone hearing it. Therefore, it must be read aloud with the same kind of emphasis, changes in tone, and variations in speed that people use in their speaking. Otherwise the person listening to the reader will have a hard time adjusting to what is said; most people won't take the extra trouble to do this, and the message will be lost.

Therefore, the reader must try to bring out the message by his own use of voice variations.

Rating Scale
(1 is best—10 is worst)

(circle one number on each line)

1. Eye Contact with Listeners	1 2 3 4 5 6 7 8 9 10
2. Posture and Movement	1 2 3 4 5 6 7 8 9 10
3. Variations in Voice (avoiding monotone)	1 2 3 4 5 6 7 8 9 10
4. Rate of Speaking	1 2 3 4 5 6 7 8 9 10
5. Voice Pitch (high or low)	1 2 3 4 5 6 7 8 9 10
6. Force (volume and energy)	1 2 3 4 5 6 7 8 9 10
7. Enunciation (clear pronounciation)	1 2 3 4 5 6 7 8 9 10
8. Use of Microphone (if available)	1 2 3 4 5 6 7 8 9 10
9. General Understandability	1 2 3 4 5 6 7 8 9 10
10. Overall Effectiveness	1 2 3 4 5 6 7 8 9 10

*Total Number:*_____
(10 is highest—100 is lowest)

Liturgy preparation. It should be evident from the previous pages of this book that planning liturgical celebrations is the *raison d'etre* for a community worship committee. The other goals or purposes sketched above are indeed significant, but ultimately they should lead to, find meaning in, and help achieve carefully prepared liturgies. The first concern in this preparation centers on all the Sunday Masses, then the other major sacramental celebrations of baptism, marriage, penance, funerals, and, finally, those special occasions like First Communion, confirmation, or Thanksgiving.

The chapters which follow will examine the liturgical services which surround spiritual rebirth, marriage, conversion, and death. We conclude this portion with an outline of how to plan eucharistic celebrations for either Sundays or weekdays.

C. Planning A Mass

The time and energy expended in preparation for a Mass will naturally depend upon the importance of each occasion. Every Eucharist, of course, deserves reverence and care, that goes without saying, but men place more emphasis on some events than on others, and the solemnity of the liturgical celebration will or should correspond to that value judgment. We will spend more effort on Sunday Masses than on weekday ones, on the Solemn Profession of Final Vows for a girl in the parish than on a home Eucharist for several couples. Certain of the following steps will, accordingly, be omitted for simpler, less formal circumstances.

The parish worship committee in preparing liturgies should keep minutes of its deliberations and maintain a ledger with its decisions, especially for the Sunday celebrations. This will eliminate overlapping and repetition. It also will enable a commission to chart the flow of ideas, to plan more intelligently, and to view the weekly themes from a wider, longer-range vantage point.

Determine a theme. The General Instruction offers considerable latitude in selecting the texts for Mass. Chapters 7 and 8 contain the principles to be observed in this regard. However, the worship committee should first examine the texts assigned to a given day, particularly those designated for Sundays. The revised Lectionary is a product of serious scholarship and the various cycles of scriptural readings have been fashioned with care. In all fairness we should test these excerpts in practice and not peremptorily criticize or reject them. However, in special circumstances it is permissible, even desirable, to choose biblical passages other than ones specifically provided as long as they can be found in the Lectionary.[7] Since that official book includes almost any reading from the Bible one would want, the worship committee enjoys here almost unrestricted freedom.

Planners will find the *Lectionary for Mass*[8] a useful aid in agreeing on a theme and arranging scriptural texts to accompany it. A swift glance at the detailed tables in the back of this paperback easily indicates if and where an individual passage can be located. The committee in charge of a Eucharist either checks the assigned readings and evolves a theme from them or conceives a unique motif for the celebration and proceeds to search for excerpts which will express or support that special concept. For example, I would like to think the worship committee might, for Sundays, study the three texts and then arrive at some theme which flows from these readings and fits the season, the circumstances of the parish, or the events of the moment. Thus, Mother's Day, the fall opening of a religious education program, a national concern which grips the attention of all may prompt an idea or notion that can be easily linked to the proper scriptural passages. Or, to illustrate a different approach, the community may wish to celebrate in a home or classroom with a small group on some weekday. Those responsible would discuss the purpose of their gathering, agree on some common theme or themes, and then refer to Bible and Lectionary for suitable texts.

My reluctance to drop the appointed readings too quickly in favor of freely chosen excerpts rests on a fear that we will, in the process, fail to catch that picture of salvation history which the reformed Lectionary seeks to paint. Moreover, without some vigilance and thought those who plan liturgies may slip into repetitive celebrations of favorite, but soon overworked, themes.

In any event, preparation of a liturgy begins with a determination of the motif or theme and a selection of apposite scriptural passages.[9]

Choose the alternatives. In some instances, notably Sundays and major feasts, the prayers (opening, over the gifts, after Communion) are already determined. But when options exist (frequently), the worship committee should attempt to pick those which reinforce the fundamental theme. Besides the prayers already cited, these include, for example, the greeting, penitential rite, responsorial psalm, alleluia verse, preface, Eucharistic Prayer, memorial acclamation, and dismissal.

Some uncomplicated communication medium must be established between committee and celebrants. Unless the priests know what decisions have been made, the liturgy will very probably be a hesitating, confused mess. On the other hand, if each celebrant goes his own way, the congregation usually suffers. For instance, when priests alternate Sunday after Sunday at the 10:15 Mass, how do you insure that the people regularly at this service hear a variety of Eucharistic Prayers? By design or accident, participants at the celebration may see different faces, but listen only to Eucharistic Prayer II. Or how will various preachers integrate the meticulously developed theme into their homilies? The Cincinnati booklet for "Parish Liturgical Commissions" offers two sample fill-in planning schedules. These surely will help; in fact they are nearly indispensable. But, as I have stated in preceding chapters, the system of one homilist covering all the Masses on a rotating basis, in my estimation, is the most workable solution.

Compose the desired texts. These brief, succinct comments or phrases lead to the scriptural readings and homily, emphasize the main theme, and remind worshipers of that motif just before they depart. They include, among others, an introduction after the greeting, terse comments before the biblical passages ("John F. Kennedy urged us to strive for excellence. So does God today through St. Paul's words. Listen."), an invitation and concluding prayer to the General Intercessions, a commentary prior to the preface, and some final remarks at the dismissal.

Such texts, composed by celebrant or committee for a specific liturgical service, are invaluable as a supplement to the homily and biblical readings. However, some variation is also in order for them. Regardless of how original or pertinent the commentary, if we always and at every Mass and in the same spot insert a few remarks, the comments soon begin to lose their impact. The committee with alert eyes and ears will quickly sense when the pattern has become routine and requires minor revamping.

Of unique importance is the General Intercession or Prayer of the Faithful. Ideally, this should be composed on the local scene, reflect the current needs of the world, nation, community, and parish, and connect with the Mass's theme and the homilist's message. The commercially prepared General Intercessions certainly may serve as a crutch for a parish or celebrant unwilling or unable to fashion suitable introductions, intentions, and conclusions. These, however, necessarily must be written and published months in advance and cannot, obviously, speak of events which develop a few days before the Sunday celebration and are very much on the minds of parishioners. More desirable, I think, is the procedure observed by the clergy of St. Thomas Parish in Cornwall-on-Hudson. Every Saturday morning one of the priests prepares a Prayer of the Faithful for the next day, a General Intercession which truly mirrors the immediate concerns of men not only in that New York State community, but throughout the entire world.

A spontaneous General Intercession works quite well in small groups, but encounters serious obstacles in larger congregations. In the latter, few can hear the quietly voiced petition of each person. Furthermore, the intentions tend to become the expression of individual requests, rather than the community's prayer for all men, all congregations, all levels of society. These personal pleas would be better left to pauses during the Eucharistic Prayer which permit a silent or vocal mention of the living and deceased.

Prepare the music. The musical program should expand or emphasize in song and word the specific theme. Moreover, the committee obviously must keep in mind the tastes of a congregation and attempt to plan the celebration so that musically speaking it will, as we recommended earlier, be varied, but comfortable, fresh, but familiar. We have in the revised Order of Mass a certain priority of occasions for congregational singing. The Sanctus, memorial acclamation, and "Amen" before the Lord's Prayer, for example, hold positions of eminence and, whenever possible, should be sung. A community worship committee would do well to examine and follow the recommendations of two documents: a statement of the Bishops' Committee on the Liturgy, "The Place of Music in Eucharistic Celebrations," and an excellent article by Father William Bauman which appeared in *Overtones*, the publication of the National Music Educators Association. Both are easily obtainable as reprints.[10] These are probably the best and the most practical contemporary texts we have on music in the liturgy.

Arrange supplementary actions. We lump in this section all the other incidentals which contribute to a well-prepared, nicely executed and potentially effective, liturgical celebration. This covers such items as an offertory procession, well-groomed ushers, colorful banners, and locally printed participation aids.

The worship committee or some division of it could handle details of weekly offertory processions. Designating ushers as bearers of gifts to the altar after the collection is a sure and easy method of accomplishing this. But in doing so we miss a golden opportunity to involve countless parishioners in a truly symbolic action of the Mass. At the Cathedral in Tucson an entire family — three generations sometimes — carries the collection, the bread and wine and chalice, and a personal gift of its own to the sanctuary. In tiny parishes, advance assignment like this of willing families to the offertory procession means that a minimum of over fifty would participate during a year's time. In larger communities we simply multiply that by the number of Sunday Masses and come up with an impressive total.

Recently, those in charge of liturgy at the Grand Rapids Cathedral stressed giving thanks on Thanksgiving through giving gifts for the poor. Publicizing the event several Sundays beforehand, the priests urged everyone to bring some concrete offering for the indigent up to the altar at the usual time. A capacity crowd filled the church for this special holiday Mass and a steady stream of offerers brought forth two dozen bushel baskets full of food for the needy.

The ushers in Tucson's Cathedral are well-dressed, wear standardized jackets with name tags, and perform their duties in a very dignified fashion. Friendly ushers (usherettes?) who greet people at the door and assist them through the service become more than collection takers and bulletin distributors. However, a word of caution: parishioners may accept direction from a priest, but resent it from an usher; praise the friendliness of the clergy, but call it boldness on the part of ushers. Considerable tact and discretion is in order lest eager ushers consciously or otherwise overdo. The parish worship committee hardly wants to become a grievance committee which checks out the complaints of women who claim they suffer from ushers the same treatment on the way to Communion that pretty girls have been rumored to receive on crowded buses in Italy.

Perhaps the most visible innovation in the reformed liturgy over the past decade has been the extensive use of colorful banners. These can be employed to illustrate the Mass's theme, the season of the Church year, the gifts presented at offertory time, the intentions of the General Intercessions. In truth they may express visually almost any concept which occurs in the celebration.

At St. Francis Church in Finleyville, Pennsylvania, a special committee of the worship committee supervises the design, creation, and placement of banners. About thirty persons in the parish have shared in this work and already have produced over fifty banners which can be selected as the occasion dictates. New ones are constantly being produced. Those who participated in the public Masses at the National C.Y.O. Convention in Denver during November 1969, will remember well how still the mammoth auditorium became when youth delegates carried symbolic gifts for the poor to the altar accompanied by students with lengthy banners depicting the offerings and their meaning. These were fixed in the sanctuary for the Eucharistic Prayer and quietly told of student involvement both in the celebration itself and in the mission of service to others which that liturgy encouraged.

Selecting the most suitable participation aids for Sunday services (and other celebrations) is a final, but extremely vital function of the worship committee. Myriad principles and judgments enter into this discussion. Hymnal or missalette? Texts with the readings and Eucharistic Prayers or without them? Make up leaflets for each Sunday or purchase commercial ones? Reproduce the words of music without seeking copyright permission or dip into the budget and pay for the right to these materials? I can see a moment in the not too distant future when a large parish with a talented and active worship committee will decide to assemble and publish its own participation-aid leaflet. It will contain only the texts needed for the people's response in word and song plus some introductory material as an explanation of the day's theme. Blessed Sacrament Parish in Alexandria, Virginia, has already undertaken such an experiment, but it would be premature at this writing to evaluate the commercial viability and practical success of that venture.

These suggested avenues or areas of concern in no way exhaust the possible approaches a parish worship committee can take in planning the liturgy. The goal before this committee is to prepare high quality, varied liturgical celebrations which make maximum use of local talent and prove satisfying to the greatest number of parishioners. It is for all of God's People — clergy, religious, laity — on the liturgy committee to find ways of achieving that sublime, but elusive goal.

Chapter 2

BORN AGAIN

The Vatican Council Fathers gave specific directions for reform of the baptismal ritual.[1] First of all baptism was to be placed in a context of Christian initiation, closely combined with confirmation and the Eucharist "to bring the faithful to the full stature of Christ and to enable them to carry out the mission of the entire people of God in the Church and in the world."[2]

More precisely, experts were to revise adult baptism, both the simpler service and the more solemn celebration. In addition a totally new ceremony for adult converts already validly baptized was to be drawn up which would indicate that the recipients had now been admitted into communion with the Church. The text also decreed that these authorities in the liturgy should create a ritual designed particularly for infants (until the present none had existed), one more sharply delineating the role of parents and godparents. Moreover, the reformers were to make provision for baptism within Mass, for blessing baptismal water by a shorter formula at each service outside Eastertime, and for baptizing a large number on one occasion.

At the moment of writing, we have available in Latin and an authorized English translation, "The Introduction to Christian Initiation and the Various Rites of Baptism for Children." The latter section follows a standard pattern of all the restored liturgical books and contains numerous options, especially with regard to prayers, readings, and blessings. By the time these words appear in print, it is most probable that the remaining baptismal rituals—for adults—will have been issued by the Congregation for Divine Worship with a vernacular version for English-speaking nations soon to follow.

This chapter will examine some central features of the infant baptismal ceremony and the theological notions behind them, then offer a few pastoral suggestions for effective use of the rite.

A. A Theology of Baptism

Perhaps the easiest way to grasp some of the theology inherent in the sacrament of baptism and to appreciate the restored service itself would be to discuss briefly new or substantially altered facets of this initiation ritual.

1. *The role of parents.* In earlier days the function of parents at a child's baptism was very limited. The mother normally remained at home preparing for the party to begin when all returned from church; the father sometimes appeared for the ceremony. The religious service, however, was the responsibility of godparents and belonged mainly to them.

This revised rite radically departs from that procedure. "Because of natural relationships, parents have a more important ministry and role in the baptism of infants than the godparents."[3] "Therefore," the text declares, "it is very important that the parents should be present in the celebration in which their child is reborn in water and the Holy Spirit."[4] Not only ought father and mother attend their baby's Christian initiation, they "have special parts to play!"

> They listen to the words addressed to them by the celebrant, they join in prayer along with the congregation, and

they exercise a special function when: a) they publicly ask that the child be baptized; b) they sign their child with the sign of the cross after the celebrant; c) they renounce Satan and make their profession of faith; d) they (and especially the mother) carry the child to the font; e) they hold the lighted candle; f) they are blessed with the special prayers for the mothers and fathers.[5]

These parental duties do not end with this final blessing by the officiating priest. Presenting a child for baptism means the acceptance of an ongoing duty to form this new Christian in his freshly received faith.

After baptism it is the responsibility of the parents, in their gratitude to God and in fidelity to the duty they have undertaken, to enable the child to know God, whose adopted child it has become, to receive confirmation, and to participate in the holy eucharist.[6]

2. *A sacrament of faith.* Baptism is not a magical service which somehow saves any and all persons regardless of inner dispositions. It is, "above all, the sacrament of that faith by which men and women, enlightened by the Spirit's grace, respond to the gospel of Christ."[7] Infants naturally cannot respond with a personal act of faith to the Lord's gift and his love. Nevertheless:

From the earliest times, the Church, to which the mission of preaching the gospel and of baptizing was entrusted, has baptized children as well as adults. Our Lord said: "Unless a man is reborn in water and the Holy Spirit, he cannot enter the kingdom of God." The Church has always understood these words to mean that children should not be deprived of baptism, because they are baptized in the faith of the Church. This faith is proclaimed for them by their parents and godparents, who represent both the local Church and the whole society of saints and believers. . . ."[8]

It is, therefore, the Church's faith which parents and godparents carry in their hearts to the font and proclaim in the name of the infant about to be plunged into the waters and born again. Their proclamation and promise entails responsibilities which continue after the child's baptism until he attains maturity.

> To fulfill the true meaning of the sacrament, children must later be formed in the faith in which they have been baptized. The foundation of this formation will be the sacrament itself, which they have already received. Christian formation, which is their due, seeks to lead them gradually to learn God's plan in Christ, so that they may ultimately accept for themselves the faith in which they have been baptized.[9]

The reception portion of the ceremony strongly brings out these two concepts of parental responsibility and the faith element of baptism. With mother presumably holding the child, husband at her side, and godparents flanking both of them, the celebrant inquires, "What do you ask of God's Church for your child?" The parents respond: "Baptism." In these or similar words the priest warns or reminds them of the serious consequences bound up with such a request:

> You have asked to have your child baptized. In doing so you are accepting the responsibility of training him (her) in the practice of the faith. It will be your duty to bring him (her) up to keep God's commandments as Christ taught us, by loving God and our neighbor. Do you clearly understand what you are undertaking?[10]

After the parents reply, "We do," the godparents hear a similar admonition and request. "Are you ready to help the parents of this child in their duty as Christian parents?" Only after they accept does he sign the child and welcome him into the Christian community.

One could presume from all this that unless the parents do believe and/or are willing to raise the infant as a Christian, the sacrament should be postponed.

3. *Service of the Word.* We have frequently mentioned throughout this book the multipresence of Christ in liturgical

celebrations. He is truly present in the Word and, later, in sacrament or sign. The purpose of a scriptural service in baptism (as in marriage, anointing, etc.) is to bring Christ in our midst through the biblical reading(s), to awaken, increase, foster our faith, and to lead us to recognize more deeply his unique presence in the sacramental pouring of water and the saying of words.

The new rite of infant baptism observes the common structure designed for all liturgical celebrations in the revised texts. First we assemble as a community (reception of the child); then we hear the Lord's message and respond in prayer (celebration of God's Word); next we perform the sacramental action itself (celebration of the sacrament); finally, we conclude the ceremony with a blessing and dismissal (conclusion of the rite).

There are in the official ritual the usual abundance of alternative readings from which to choose — Old Testament (3), New Testament (6), Gospels (12). In addition, the ritual provides a series of responsorial psalms and verses before the gospel. It is for the celebrant, working, whenever feasible, with the family to select one or two or a few of these biblical excerpts for the Word service.

4. *Welcome into the community.* The faith received by the child is a gift from God, of course, as supernatural belief must always be, but it likewise remains a gift from the Church, which recognizes parents as the instruments that transmit this divine donation. The ceremony of baptism, consequently, welcomes, initiates, accepts, receives the candidate into a community of believing Christians, the Church.

> Further, baptism is the sacrament by which men and women are incorporated into the Church, built into a house where God lives, in the Spirit, into a holy nation and a royal priesthood. It is a sacramental bond of unity linking all who have been signed by it. Because of that unchangeable effect (signified in the Latin liturgy by the anointing of the baptized person with the chrism in the presence of God's people), the rite of baptism is held in highest honor by all Christians. It may never lawfully be repeated, once it has

> been validly celebrated, even if by fellow Christians from whom we are separated.[11]

The rite itself seeks to teach this truth by actively involving as many as possible in the service.

> In the actual celebration, the people of God (represented not only by the parents, godparents and relatives, but also, as far as possible, by friends, neighbors, and some members of the local church) should take an active part. Thus they will show their common faith and express their joy as the newly baptized are received into the community of the Church.[12]
>
> The people of God, that is the Church, made present in the local community, has an important part to play in the baptism of both children and adults.[13]

Such participation comes in many places throughout the celebration. All present respond to petitions of the General Intercession and the litany of saints, all lend their support to invocations over the water, all give their assent to the profession of faith ("This is our faith. This is the faith of the Church. We are proud to profess it, in Christ Jesus our Lord."), all pray the Lord's Prayer, all add an affirming "Amen" after prayers and blessings, all present are blessed at the conclusion in this way:

> By God's gift, through water and the Holy Spirit, we are reborn to everlasting life. In his goodness, may he continue to pour out his blessings upon all present, who are his sons and daughters. May he make them always, wherever they may be, faithful members of his holy people. May he send his peace upon all who are gathered here, in Christ Jesus our Lord.[14]

Perhaps the most lucid and explicit demonstration of this welcome concept of baptism comes at the introductory or reception rite of the liturgy. Having interrogated parents and godparents about their willingness to assume responsibility for the child's religious upbringing, the celebrant continues:

> N., the Christian community welcomes you with great joy.
> In its name I claim you for Christ our Savior by the sign of
> his cross. I now trace the cross on your forehead, and invite
> your parents (and godparents) to do the same.[15]

This fivefold silent signing of the child speaks powerfully in
practice about the baby as a newly welcomed member of the
Christian Church about to rise with Jesus through the saving
water of baptism.

5. *Fresh water.* Most readers on some past occasion probably
have noted a baptismal font with rather dirty-looking water and
an ugly scum circling the sides of the bowl. The parish priest
may be faulted for maintaining such an unattractive, unclean
baptistry, but, in truth, he labored under a severe handicap — the
necessary use of oil-saturated water preserved in certain instances for use through an entire year after the Holy Saturday
blessing.

The renewed rite drastically alters that practice. Baptismal
water should be true water, clean, heated when necessary, and
fresh for each ceremony except during the Easter season.[16]

> Except in the case of necessity, the priest or deacon should
> use only water that has been blessed for the rite. The water
> consecrated at the Easter Vigil should, if possible, be kept
> and used throughout the Easter season to signify more
> clearly the relationship between the sacrament of baptism
> and the paschal mystery. Outside the Easter season, it is
> desirable that the water be blessed for each occasion, in
> order that the words of blessing may clearly express the
> mystery of salvation which the Church recalls and pro-
> claims. If the baptistry is supplied with flowing water, the
> blessing will be given to the water as it flows.[17]

One can readily recall many instances in which God has used
water to save, cleanse, heal his People in the course of salvation history. It was the walls of water in Exodus which delivered
the Jews from pagan bondage in Egypt. It was water God used

with Noah to purify an evil generation. It was with water that the Chosen Ones were to fulfill the prescribed ceremonial washings. It was in water that John baptized and called for a conversion from sin to a life of holiness. It is by water and the Holy Spirit that Jesus did and does save us.

Each of the three blessings and invocations of God over the water refer to some of these cases in which the Father has employed this basic element in his actions with men.

Fresh, flowing water is encouraged for baptism; so, too, immersion, symbolizing the dying and rising, the being buried with Christ and the coming forth to a new life notion of this sacrament, receives preferential rating in the directives.[18] St. Richard's Church in Jackson, Mississippi, contains a large font at its entrance with this type of flowing water which also facilitates baptism by immersion.

6. *The paschal mystery.* If we wished to select one theme which recurs throughout each of the restored liturgical books, it would be this—the Easter mystery, the paschal concept of Jesus' dying, rising, and coming again. The simplification of the Church calendar, the amplified readings, the General Instruction, the anointing and funeral rites, in fact all of the reformed texts take as starting point and ultimate goal this paschal mystery and the faithful's greater participation in it. The baptismal service, since it first and perhaps most forcefully plunges us into this saving event, naturally reverberates with this concept. The General Introduction to Christian Initiation, speaking about baptism's dignity, says all this succinctly and well.

> Far superior to the purifications of the old law, baptism produces all these effects by the power of the mystery of the Lord's passion and resurrection. Those who are baptized are engrafted in the likeness of Christ's death. They are buried with him, they are given life again with him, and with him they rise again. For baptism recalls and effects the paschal mystery itself, because by means of it men and women pass from the death of sin into life. Its celebration, therefore, should reflect the joy of the resurrection, especially when it takes place during the Easter Vigil or on a Sunday.[19]

The large Easter candle, situated in the sanctuary during paschal time as a sign of the Risen Lord and moved to the baptistry for the balance of the year, clearly denotes the intimate connection between the waters of baptism and the paschal mystery. Liturgical experts recommend that each child have a personal candle for the service. After the infant's rebirth in water, the father (or someone from the family) takes this special candle and lights it from the burning paschal wick. "Receive the light of Christ" are the celebrant's words and, later, he reminds all present that "This child of yours has been enlightened by Christ."[20] What kind of commitment for parent and child this implies has been described at length above. However, some reminder of that particular part of the liturgy for baptism could be helpful in the ensuing years and we will mention a way of doing so in the second section of this chapter.

7. *Baptism and the Eucharist.* Baptism introduces a child into the community of Christian believers and readies an infant for the reception of confirmation and the Eucharist, the two complementary rites of initiation. This sacrament, then, is deeply linked to eucharistic celebrations, liturgies which form the core of worship for us, and where the Church primarily happens or becomes.

The restored ritual brings out that relationship several times in the service. For example, the movement after the actual baptism from font to altar for the concluding rite clearly teaches this. Moreover, the common recitation of the Lord's Prayer at that point likewise illustrates the orientation of baptism to the Eucharist. From earliest Christian days, the Church had employed the Our Father in any liturgy which involves the Eucharist and sees in phrases like "our daily bread" an implied reference to the bread of heaven which gives men eternal life. The celebrant, standing in front of the altar and inviting the whole assembly to pray this Our Father, expresses all of these notions. In the following or similar words, he says:

> Dearly beloved, these children have been reborn in baptism. They are now called children of God, for so indeed they are. In confirmation they will receive the fullness of

> God's spirit. In holy communion they will share the
> banquet of Christ's sacrifice, calling God their Father in the
> midst of the Church. In their name, in the Spirit of our com-
> mon sonship, let us pray together in the words our Lord has
> given us.[21]

Finally, the official text remarks: "On Sunday, baptism may be celebrated even during Mass, so that the entire community may be present and the necessary relationship between baptism and the eucharist may be clearly seen but this should not be done too often."[22] It outlines the procedure as well. The reception of children replaces the greeting and penitential rite; a liturgy of the word with reading, homily, General Intercessions but no Creed follows the opening prayer; the celebration of baptism proper resumes at the prayer of exorcism and continues through to, but excluding the concluding rite; the celebrant returns to the Mass at the offertory and, for the final blessing, may use one of the solemn baptismal benedictions.[23]

8. *Exorcism.* One of the incongruities in the older rite used for infant baptism (but originally designed for adults) and something offensive to many was the harsh terminology which spoke of the tiny tot as infected with or possessed by the devil. Many priests particularly found it objectionable and uncomfortable to blow gently on the face of an innocent baby and command: "Depart from him (her), unclean spirit. . . ." or to pray, "Free him (her) from the snares of Satan which until now have held them."[24] To address, albeit indirectly, this helpless child with the words "accursed and damned spirit" bothered them. The totally new ritual for the baptism of children corrects this, especially in the alternative form for the prayer of exorcism.

> Almighty God,
> you sent your only Son
> to rescue us from the slavery of sin,
> and to give us the freedom
> only your sons and daughters enjoy.
>
> We now pray for these children
> who will have to face the world with its temptations,
> and fight the devil in all his cunning.

Your Son died and rose again to save us.
By his victory over sin and death,
bring these children out of the power of darkness.
Strengthen them with the grace of Christ,
and watch over them at every step in life's journey.[25]

9. *Blessing of parents.* We used to "church" mothers after childbirth, giving those devout women who came to the baptismal service and requested it, a special blessing after the ceremony. The prayers were meaningful enough, but the ritual seemed anticlimactic, awkward (mother holding child and candle), came at a poor time (after a full morning and following a lengthy liturgy of baptism with perhaps a half dozen infants), and reached only a few of the "saved." The present ritual improves this greatly by incorporating a blessing of mothers, fathers, and all present in the conclusion of the baptism. We already have cited one of the benedictions for the congregation. This formula for mothers exemplifies simplicity and directness:

> May God, the source of life and love, who fills the hearts of mothers with love for their children, bless the mothers of these newly-baptized children. As they thank God for a safe delivery, may they find joy in the love, growth, and holiness of their children.[26]

There are, as usual, alternative versions.

Since the fathers had something to do with all of this, the final blessings include several invocations like the one below.

> God is the giver of all life, human and divine. May he bless the fathers of these children. With their wives they will be the first teachers of their children in the ways of faith. May they be also the best of teachers, bearing witness to the faith by what they say and do, in Christ Jesus our Lord.[27]

B. Practical Suggestions

The revised rite for infant baptism has not been in use long enough to offer us the fruit of actual experience or the extensive pastoral suggestions for its implementation on the practical level. The few recommendations outlined here may serve as starters.

1. *Preparation classes.* The directives of this ritual call for proper preparation of families and a common celebration on the same day. In fact the norms even specify, "except for a good reason, baptism should not be celebrated more than once on the same day in the same church."[28] Sundays or during the Easter Vigil when the Church commemorates the Lord's resurrection are mentioned as preferred dates since this should emphasize the paschal character of baptism.[29] These ideals, however, create two difficulties, both involving time—how to prepare a dozen families adequately in a few weeks and how to celebrate a baptismal liturgy which does not run on for an excessively long period.

Some parishes already have resolved these problems through instructional classes a week in advance of the baptism. At this session the priest completes the mechanical arrangements and obtains the informational details needed, such as names of children, parents, godparents, addresses, dates, etc. But more importantly he fulfills the responsibilities imposed upon him through these words of the ritual:

> It is the duty of the priest to prepare families for the baptism of their children and to help them in the task of Christian formation which they have undertaken.[30]
>
> It is also the duty of the priest to arrange that baptism is always celebrated with proper dignity and, as far as possible, adapted to the circumstances and wishes of the families concerned.[31]
>
> Before the celebration of the sacrament, it is of great importance that parents, moved by their own faith or with the help of friends or other members of the community, should prepare to take part in the rite with understanding. They should be provided with suitable means such as books, instructions, and catechisms written for families. The parish priest should make it his duty to visit them, or see that they are visited, as a family or as a group of families, and prepare them for the coming celebration by pastoral counsel and common prayer.[32]

During a one-hour Saturday afternoon or weekday evening class the priest distributes booklets on baptism and participation aids for the ceremony, shows a filmstrip or movie on the sacrament, lectures about the responsibilities of parents toward the Christian education of the children, and with the parents and godparents prepares for the liturgy.

The potential of such gatherings for goodwill and catechetical instruction should be obvious.

2. *Parental involvement.* Such preparation sessions make more thorough parental involvement possible. Texts can be selected, readers assigned, the Prayer of the Faithful and litany developed, songs chosen and rehearsed. Since all these elements are cared for in the advance class, the actual service will begin on time, move quickly, and those present can participate actively and with much greater understanding.

One priest has used this as a springboard to engage the older children in a dialogue homily during the baptism. He asks them questions about water, the candle, the oil, and even seeks from the parents an explanation of why they chose certain texts and what baptism means to them.

3. *Concelebration of the sacrament.* "The celebrant may be assisted by other priests and deacons and also by the laity in those parts which pertain to them, especially if there are many persons to be baptized."[33] Preparation sessions eliminate much of the unnecessary delays before and during the service. But even with that economy of time, the liturgy for ten or twenty babies may seem interminable, especially to the mothers who stand holding the infant throughout the celebration.

At Sacred Heart Church in Troy, New York, all priests of the parish celebrate every baptism in the manner described above. They assist with certain parts (anointing, baptizing), which substantially shortens the service. In addition, their vocal support and the presence of the organist encourages the congregation to sing or respond at appropriate moments. This enhances the celebration, "stimulates a sense of unity among those present. . . , gives warmth to their common prayer, and. . . expresses the joy of Easter."[34]

Chairs for the mothers at baptisms in Sacred Heart have solved the other difficulty, easing the women's burden and enabling them to concentrate on the meaning of the liturgy, rather than the weariness in their legs.

4. *Baptism within Mass.* An occasional baptism within Mass is a potent catechetical instrument. It teaches parishioners the meaning of this sacrament and underscores its eucharistic orientation. However, as the guidelines note, the practice should not be too frequent.

St. Joseph's in Middle River, Minnesota, typifies the small, rural parish. Father Donald Krebs officiates at relatively few baptisms during the year and generally does so in the context of a Sunday eucharistic celebration. With large urban or suburban units, obviously such a policy is not feasible. Even in those instances, however, a rotating schedule could give regular worshipers at a specific Mass an occasional experience of baptism performed within the Eucharist.

5. *Communal celebration.* "So that baptism may clearly appear as the sacrament of the Church's faith and of admittance into the people of God, it should normally be celebrated in the parish church. . . ."[35] This is also the reason for the prohibition, except in danger of death, against baptismal celebrations in private houses. One might also see this, however, as a protection from favoritism toward the affluent. The rich might well want to use their comfortable home for baptism; I would think the poor might feel less anxious to have the service in their crowded one-room apartment.

Combining the baptism of one or a few infants into the larger celebration for many each month has been the manner in which some parishes have attempted to provide a larger congregation and a more suitable communal service. This procedure naturally harmonizes well with the practice of those preparation classes we treated earlier.

6. *Anniversary of baptism.* Most people recall their birthdays, but not so many remember the dates of their baptisms. A small

domestic celebration held each year at the main meal certainly would fix the day firmly in a child's mind and perhaps, later, assist him in making the mature, personal act of faith which parents make in his name at baptism.

The Will and Baumer Candle Company has reprinted an article from the August 1970, issue of *Homiletic and Pastoral Review* as a leaflet to accompany the special baptismal candle.[36] The six-page folder contains a brief explanation of baptism, the paschal mystery and the candle, plus an anniversary service to be conducted at home by one of the parents, the godparents, or someone in a similar position. With the candle lighted for this renewal ceremony, the child (the parents for him during the first years) renews vows made at baptism. Such a yearly observation would speak silently to the child for a while; later, however, this should impress upon him the date of his baptism and what it means to be born again of water and the Holy Spirit.

Chapter 3

TO LOVE AND HONOR
EACH OTHER
ALL THE DAYS OF OUR LIVES

Tiny Tim and his youthful bride invited the whole nation, perhaps the entire world to their wedding. Relatives, friends, and interested Americans needed only to flip a television switch, turn to the Johnny Carson Show, and watch the ceremony. The time, the place, the ritual itself represented a break from tradition, from procedures minutely described in books of etiquette. Some surely judged this a mere publicity stunt, as crass, commercial exploitation of a sacred event for the sake of cash. Many others, however, viewed the unusual proceedings in a quite different light. They saw in this unorthodox exchange of nuptial vows a mirror of the modern mentality.

Today an increasing number of men and women about to promise love, honor, and loyalty in good times and in bad, in sickness and in health all the days of their lives wish to add a personal note to these serious and solemn commitments. Couples like that want to do their own thing, to fashion a celebration which bears the stamp of their unique personalities. They are not particularly concerned about the conventional rules which grandparents, parents, brothers or sisters followed before them.

167

So they write their own service, select for the rite Central Park in New York or a pretty spot under cherry blossoms in the Tidal Basin at Washington or a sandy location by the ocean at Pacific Palisades in California, and start a life of love together.

The revised Roman Catholic marriage ritual came, then, at a most providential time. Its multiple options, its many scriptural readings, prayers, blessings, its emphasis on the couple planning the ceremony perfectly suits the temperament of most engaged people. They may not opt for the radical departure from convention of a Tiny Tim or of the bride and groom in *Alice's Restaurant*, but they do welcome an opportunity to prepare their own wedding. Until recent months the prospective spouses spent days over invitation lists, details of the rehearsal party or reception dinner, and arrangements for the honeymoon. The religious ceremony, however, remained a strict prerogative of the officiating priest.

We fortunately now face a totally different approach. After only a few months the testimony seems remarkably clear—the vast majority of men and women are delighted with the possibilities of the reformed ritual, give long hours to joint study of the texts, practice shared decision-making with the alternatives, even compose a personal prayer, and publish their own participation booklet for the guest. It is, in my estimation, a remarkable sign of seriousness and a real cause of hope for the future when bride and groom read and ponder twenty-eight biblical passages about matrimony in preparation for the nuptial service.

A dose of renewed enthusiasm for the battered institution of marriage wouldn't harm anyone these days. The care with which the engaged prepare their solemn celebration of a marital commitment may act as an antidote to the pervading pessimistic mood about matrimony which surrounds us. High divorce rates and the example of some who continue to live together, but obviously no longer love each other, strike fear, doubt, and anxiety in the hearts of at least a few contemplating marriage. They ask: Should we risk this adventure? Do we really love one another? Will we end up like our parents, our friends, our relatives? Why marry at all? Why not just live together, try it out, make a temporary commitment?

Occasional writers pick up these questions and interpret them as the final gasps of a dying institution. Nicholas von Hoffman, who regularly assails "sacred cows" and unassailable gods of the Establishment in his column for the Washington *Post*, recently directed some of his acid-tipped arrows at matrimony. He wrote in "Divorcing Marriage":

> Faith in the traditional Western European marriage has been dying a long death. An increasingly large number of people just don't think they can make it in holy matrimony; the ideal of matching up with somebody in the early 20's and sticking together happily for 40 or 50 years seems unattainable.[1]

The movies from Hollywood reflect to some extent what men and women in Pueblo, Colorado; Finley, Ohio; and Brewster, Massachusetts, are thinking or talking about and doing. One Los Angeles film critic, discussing "A Mess of Movies Look at the Mess of Marriage," commented on this trend:

> Having spent more than half a century persuading us that an endless succession of Theys lived happily ever after, the movies almost as one have now coughed nervously, toed the deep-pile wall-to-wall carpet, averted our gaze and confessed that that isn't quite the whole story.
>
> In fact, it's hard to remember a recent movie which dared to suggest that the couple would live happily through next weekend, let alone ever after. Like our society, the movies are taking a hard and worried look at marriage weighing it and finding it less wanted than it used to be.[2]

In this kind of a milieu, one finds refreshing a ceremony which has been carefully planned, which captures some of the personal love and expectations of bride and groom, which mixes romantic idealism with a touch of after-ten-years realism. Weddings like these are genuine experiences. They provide married guests with a shot of encouragement, bring back memories of similar moments in an earlier age, and have been known to elicit from moved onlookers a few tears, a squeeze of the hand, a tender kiss.

The many options of this flexible marriage liturgy flow from certain theological considerations. We will first examine them, then describe practical steps in planning the wedding, and, finally, offer a sample homily for the nuptial service.

A. A Theology of Marriage

In the next section we will recommend a few practices which can more deeply involve couple and congregation in the ceremony. The basis for such suggestions are truths of a doctrinal, biblical nature about marriage itself. Thus, the encouragement of a symbolic offering for the poor, as gifts are prepared and presented after the exchange of vows, rests on the deeper notion that the love in marriage should be out-going, expansive, reaching to those in need beyond the family circle. We outline here the major themes and central concepts.[3]

1. *First covenant between God and his People*

Love in marriage is a giving-receiving relationship. Just as the sacrament and state of matrimony are mysteries, so, too, the mingling of give and take between husband and wife never can be clearly defined, even by the partners themselves. Contemporary theologians today speak of these things more in terms of a nuptial covenant than the matrimonial contract. As such it parallels the covenant, the giving-receiving, the love and response situation which exists between God and his People.

The Father initiates this love affair. He first creates, loves, saves us. It is for us to respond to that never-ceasing love. He, centuries ago, promised to be our God, to protect, guard, guide, forgive, love us and make of us his chosen People. He seeks in return simply our faith, trust, love, and loyalty.

We find these notions in several parts of Sacred Scripture. In Hosea, God extends his love, promises he will be faithful and make of Israel his People even though they have been faithless.

> I will betroth you to myself with faithfulness,
> and you will come to know Yahweh.

When that day comes—it is Yahweh who speaks—
   the heavens will have their answer from me,
   the earth its answer from them,
   the grain, the wine, the oil, their answer from the
     earth,
   and Jezreel his answer from them.
I will sow him in the country,
I will love Unloved;
I will say to No-People-of-Mine, "You are my
   people,"
      and he will answer, "You are my God."[4]

The prophet Jeremiah speaks in Chapter 3 of God's People as an unfaithful spouse who will convert and return to "Yahweh our God."[5]

In Ezekiel, Chapters 16 and 23, this type of imagery continues with the Lord Yahweh clearly standing by the covenant he had earlier made with Israel.

> Lord Yahweh says this: I will treat you as you deserve, you who have despised your oath even to the extent of breaking a covenant, but I will remember the covenant that I made with you when you were a girl, and I will conclude a covenant with you that shall last for ever. And you for your part will remember your past behaviour and be covered with shame when I take your elder and younger sisters and make them your daughters, although this was not included in this covenant. I am going to renew my covenant with you; and you will learn that I am Yahweh, and so remember and be covered with shame, and in your confusion be reduced to silence, when I have pardoned you for all that you have done—it is the Lord Yahweh who speaks.[6]

Isaiah bears the same message.

> For now your creator will be your husband,
> his name, Yahweh Sabaoth;
> your redeemer will be the Holy One of Israel,
> he is called the God of the whole earth.
> Yes, like a forsaken wife, distressed in spirit,
> Yahweh calls you back.
> Does a man cast off the wife of his youth?
> says your God.[7]

The additional concept of a covenant sealed with blood, that symbol of life itself and sign of the common life between the Lord and his People, is mentioned in Exodus.

> Moses went and told the people all the commands of Yahweh and all the ordinances. In answer, all the people said with one voice, "We will observe all the commands that Yahweh had decreed." Moses put all the commands of Yahweh into writing, and early next morning he built an altar at the foot of the mountain, with twelve standing stones for the twelve tribes of Israel. Then he directed certain young Israelites to offer holocausts and to immolate bullocks to Yahweh as communion sacrifices. Half of the blood Moses took up and put into basins, the other half he cast on the altar. And taking the Book of the Covenant he read it to the listening people, and they said, "We will observe all that Yahweh has decreed; we will obey." Then Moses took the blood and cast it towards the people. "This," he said, "is the blood of the Covenant that Yahweh has made with you, containing all these rules."[8]

The same book contains Israel's response, "All that Yahweh has said, we will do,"[9] to God's invitation that they enter a loving relationship with him.

2. *Marriage between God and man*

Philippians 2 describes how Jesus emptied himself out and "became as men are." This further sign of God's love – the giving of his Son and Christ's own self-donation through becoming man – wedded the human and the divine in Jesus. Because the Lord linked within himself this world and the other, accepted all we have and are except sin, he therefore both made holy and bore witness to the fact that everything around us is basically good, including sex, love, and marriage.

3. *Second or new covenant*

Christ's love extended beyond the Incarnation. We celebrate in the Eucharistic Prayers his dying, rising, coming again, the total paschal mystery. By such total self-giving, through pouring out his Precious Blood, he renewed the old covenant and elevated it into a new one. Jesus made friendship with God a possibility once more, opened the gates of heaven, fashioned us into a Church, his Mystical Body, the new People of God. He asks in response, as before, only faith, trust, love, loyalty, and service to others.

4. *Mysterious sign*

Ephesians 5 speaks about the husband as head of the wife, but also mentions that marriage is a mystery like the Church. This sign value of matrimony works both ways. God's love for us, indicated in both Old and New Covenant biblical sources, supplies a couple with guidelines for their own marital living. If Yahweh, to illustrate, can forgive a faithless spouse, what about a contemporary husband or wife? If God can love so much, may a man or woman care to do less? Conversely, a couple deeply in love, close to one another, caring about those near them, also speaks to modern men about God. How many searching, doubting young people have found their way back to the Ultimate through this mysterious thing we call love?

5. *Marriage as a sacrament*

Christ is *the* sacrament and his Church is *the* sign of Jesus working, living, present in the world today. But the Lord has given us, in addition, seven unique sacraments to help us live Christian lives. Marriage is one of them and its essence consists of the formal vow to live and love together until death *and* the actual living out of that loving promise. It follows, consequently, that any thought, word, or act of love, including sexual intercourse, becomes a source of grace, a vehicle of Christ's presence, a sign of the Holy Spirit in married people's lives.

6. *An outgoing love*

The Dogmatic Constitution on the Church asserts, "The family is, so to speak, the domestic Church."[10] It should be a sign to all persons. A truly Christian parish must look beyond itself; a diocese, beyond its boundaries; a nation, beyond its shores. So, too, husband and wife, mother and father must reach beyond themselves, their home, their families, to others. This imposes a special obligation upon them to show care for the poor, needy, suffering, aged, lonely, and to manifest concern particularly for couples in distress and younger ones about to marry. The decree on the Apostolate of the Laity spells out the details of this responsibility.[11]

7. *Communal nature of the celebration*

Every liturgical service by its very nature is communal, a work of the entire Church, and should actively involve all participants. The nuptial ceremony, since it shares this quality of authentic liturgy, likewise possesses a communitarian nature. In addition, however, because of marriage's social implications (giving new life to the human race as well as supplying warm companionship to the two partners), the service should somehow demonstrate in a special way the involvement of the community, symbolized by the congregation, in the lives of these two people who will not only live together for life, but in society with other persons.

B. Practical Suggestions

Preparing for the wedding ceremony begins, officially, when bride and groom contact the parish to arrange a date and time for the marriage. Their initial step is a momentous one for the couple and the manner in which a priest receives their call and visit starts the process off well or poorly.

The man and woman normally have not been through this experience before, wonder what to expect, and hope the desired spot on the church calendar is not already reserved. They bubble over with enthusiasm and joy, but feel anxious, overwhelmed, tense, especially when one partner is not Roman Catholic. The cleric who welcomes them warmly, who puts them at ease, who leisurely but efficiently spells out the necessary mechanics establishes an invaluable rapport.

If he continues this contact through the prenuptial instructions, the preliminary questionnaire, the rehearsal, then by the time the formal wedding arrives both bride and groom will be quite comfortable in his presence. Such an involvement over a period of several months will enable him to add the personal touch which transforms an ordinary, even if solemn, service into a beautiful, moving experience. For these reasons it is surely desirable that the same priest handle all these functions from the earliest contact through the concluding reception. Moreover, his frequent association with the prospective partners supplies him with a better understanding of them and fuller information about their backgrounds.

The task of a priest in the revised marriage rite is, above all, to explain the various textual and ceremonial options available for a couple and to allow them the selection of those they deem the most suitable. The immediate and extensive success of *Together for Life*, a booklet designed to assist celebrant and future spouses in choosing texts, indicates that our Catholic clergy quickly accepted this procedure whereby the bride and groom plan their own wedding ceremony.[12] This publication (or one similar to it) and the companion forms for both editions provided by the publisher render it relatively easy for the couple to study scriptural readings, prayers and blessings, note their choices, and return a completed list to the celebrant. With this in his hand before the service he can mark ritual books for lectern and altar.

The reformed *Rite of Marriage* offers in addition to a variety of texts, certain ceremonial alternatives. A colored, sound filmstrip, also entitled *Together for Life*, visualizes some of these possibilities.[13] The basic kit containing this audiovisual aid includes a checklist of options for the couple to ponder over and decide upon. Having viewed that filmstrip at premarriage classes or in the course of a visit with the priest, the bride and groom should recall the ideas suggested there when they glance through these guidelines for planning the wedding. They then can build their own service, complete the form, and advise the celebrant of decisions made.

The questions which appear on this list illustrate how the filmstrip and accompanying form work in practice, what a few of the ceremonial possibilities are, and how open-ended the procedure really is.

1. *Entrance procession.* Traditional? With parents? Some other form?

2. *Order of service booklet.* Commercially prepared one? Personally composed? None?

3. *Congregational singing.* Yes? No? If yes, what arrangements have been made?

4. *Reader of first two scriptural texts.* Priest? Relative? or Friend? Who?
   Reading 1: _____
   Reading 2: _____

5. *Wedding vows.* Face the priest? The congregation? One another?

6. *Recitation of promises.* From a book? After the priest? By memory?

7. *Exchange of rings.* Single ring ceremony? Double?

8. *Prayer of the couple.* Yes? No? If so, when? After the exchange of rings? At Communion time? Some other moment? Personally composed? Prepared by other? From where?

9. *General Intercessions.* Personally composed? Prepared by priest? Who will read the petitions? You? Priest? Someone else? Who?

10. *Offertory procession.* Yes? No? Gift for the poor. Yes? No? What will it be? Who will bring the gifts to the altar?

11. *Sign of peace.* Yes? No? Just the two of you? The wedding party also? The entire congregation? How should this be done?

12. *Communion under both kinds.* Yes? No?

13. *Other ceremonies desired.* (Lengthy space provided)

It should be evident that preparation of a personal, individualized marriage ceremony takes time. The future spouses naturally must spend at least a few and probably many hours in planning the service. Moreover, the priest likewise must give extra moments (perhaps forty-five minutes) merely unveiling to the couple the multiple options open to them. When he officiates at several dozen weddings each year this repetitive explanation can become a heavy burden.

One parish in Cincinnati introduced an experimental premarriage class held every month or so which seeks to resolve that difficulty. During this evening meeting, a priest distributes the booklets, shows the filmstrip, and explains the local ground rules. In addition, he gives participants a sheet with details of the technical matters involved in contracting a marriage and planning a wedding—the license, flowers, altar boys, instructions, documents, offerings, etc. The director of music then takes over and describes some of the musical possibilities, concluding with a demonstration of sample processional, recessional and interlude pieces on the church organ. This class neither replaces diocesan pre-Cana courses nor eliminates the personal meeting of couple and celebrant. It does, nevertheless, save time, anticipate questions, and more thoroughly acquaint brides and grooms-to-be with the alternatives for their ceremony.

Couples with certain creative talents and a willingness to work seriously at the preparation of their service should find two particular aspects quite appealing: the composition of several prayers and the compilation of a participation booklet.

A Prayer of the Couple, recited by them following the nuptial promises or after Communion or at some other opportune moment, is directed to God the Father and seeks his blessing upon them and upon their marriage. *Together for Life* offers an illustration which can serve as a model for those who wish to write their own prayer (the ideal situation) or as the actual text for those who care to use a Prayer of the Couple, but prefer to employ the words of someone else.[14] Nancy Ryerse and David Smithfield spoke these phrases of the one they personally composed after exchanging vows on a June afternoon in St. Ambrose Church, Cheverly, Maryland.

> Dear God, we have come before you today in the presence
> of our parents and friends to unite ourselves to each other

as husband and wife. We ask that you bless this union. We do not know what life has in store for us. We only ask that no matter what our future holds, through your help we can continue to grow in love.

Please help me to be a loving and understanding husband to Nancy. If our marriage is blessed with children, let me love them, care for their needs, and be as good an example for them as possible. Give me the courage to be gentle when I can be and strong when I must be.

Help me to be a good wife to David. Never let me put myself or my work ahead of him. Let me find ways of always making his life happy. If you bless me with motherhood, I promise to love our children, to care for them and to be always with them when they need me.

We ask, finally, that in our old age we may love one another as deeply and cherish each other as much as we do at this very moment. May you grant these favors which we ask through your son Jesus Christ. Amen.

The General Intercessions or Prayer of the Congregation presents a similar opportunity for the imaginative couple. Once again, the booklet *Together for Life* includes a text which illustrates the standard format and even could be employed in an actual service.[15] Nevertheless, a more personal prayer of the faithful created especially for the occasion by the bride and groom is to be preferred. In my own experience, I have witnessed very few instances in which prospective spouses felt competent enough to compose these prayers, although many opted for the formula in *Together for Life*. Apparently this may require added training and further encouragement before it becomes a common practice at Catholic weddings.

Because there are so many options in the restored rite of marriage, commercial firms have found publication of an inexpensive, complete participation aid for the nuptial services a thorny problem. Some couples, in lieu of this, might assemble their own Order of Service which ushers hand to guests upon arrival at the Church. This could be a leaflet or a booklet, a simple mention of participants with an outline of the ceremony, or a full description of the service with all the responses for the congregation. In the latter case, the assistance of a priest in its preparation becomes almost imperative. Frank P. Hurley and Winifred M. Connor prepared an excellent twenty-one page mimeographed booklet for their nuptial celebration at St. Michael's Church in Spryfield, Halifax, Nova Scotia. Nancy and David's stapled, Xeroxed leaflet was more modest, containing responses for only the readings, blessings, and prayers without the texts for the Ordinary of the Mass. Richard Dali and Jerilyn Jerry created a sort of flier for their wedding at St. Thomas of Canterbury Church in Cornwall-on-Hudson, New York. The artistic cover spelled out JOY, with the "O" formed by figures of seven children in a circle holding hands. Along the "Y" were the words, "Go in Peace. Live in Love." Two inside pages listed the names of celebrants, altar boys, attendants, singers and organist, then outlined the Order of Service, mentioning specifically the musical and scriptural selections. A greeting from Dick and Jeri welcomed the guests in a few carefully chosen lines: "We would like to welcome you, our friends, to share with us this, our most beautiful day; to witness and be part of, the beginning of our lives together."

Nancy and David's introduction spelled out in more detail the background behind their booklet and the theme of their celebration.

Dear Relatives and Friends,

We both wish to welcome you to our wedding. We are glad that you could come to share in our happiness.

We spent many happy hours in planning our marriage. Part of this time was devoted to preparing this booklet. Its purpose is to provide a means by which you may participate in our marriage ceremony. We ask that you join with us in the prayers and responses to the Scripture Readings that are contained in the booklet.

The ceremony that you will participate in today reflects a little of both of us. Our theme is love. Love for each other that is being blessed today and love for our fellow man. We hope that through love, all of you have found as much happiness in your lives as we hope to find in ours.

A couple sees the moment of a marriage as *their* moment; the ceremony, *their* ceremony; the day, *their* day. And this is as it should be. The more they can be involved in the preparation of the nuptial service, the more personal, the more satisfying, the more memorable their wedding will become. However, the priest's role here, as we mentioned at the beginning of this section, is critically important. The way he first receives them, his warmth, interest, agreeableness during the instructions, the manner in which he conducts the rehearsal (with patience and humor), lays the foundation. If he does these things well, he undoubtedly will preside perfectly over the liturgy itself. The bride and groom will always remember such a celebration and they will never forget the celebrant who made it possible.

C. Homily at the Wedding

The homily at a nuptial service should be as personal as possible. The celebrant needs to integrate the readings selected and the couple's circumstances into a brief (probably no more than five minutes) message which will prepare bride, groom, and guests for the exchange of vows which follows. "Canned" wedding sermons lack this individual touch and ought to be employed only as a last resort. The text below, therefore, is merely a sample of ideas and approach.

> Today is an occasion for joy, hopes, dreams. Jim and Joan at this moment are very happy, even if a bit nervous. They feel deep joy in their hearts, have high hopes for the future, and dream of marital bliss. It may seem cruel in the midst of such elation to interject a note of reality, to remind the bride and groom of some facts about marriage, but the times call for such realism.
>
> Young couples—Jim and Joan are no exception—believe their love is true and their marriage will last. But they also have some deep fears. They know that many, too many, couples apparently lose something of their early love along the way. Something goes wrong. And a marriage, once begun as a promise and a dream to last forever, turns sour.

The two people either break up or continue on living together, but no longer loving each other. Happiness in matrimony, then, doesn't just happen; husband and wife must work at loving and living if they expect their house to be a happy home.

I would like to leave with you, Jim and Joan, three words as reminders for the years ahead. They summarize, I think, what God expects of you as husband and wife; they also contain the basic ingredients of a successful marriage.

First of all, *share.* You obviously will share many things after you leave this church. The congratulations and gifts of guests are a start; the wedding cake is a symbol. But you will and must share much more—your time, your money, your bodies, your home. But above all you need to share your feelings—the joys and sorrows, the successes and failures. You need to communicate inner feelings, to get them out of one heart into the heart of the other. When you feel neglected or angry, Jim, you somehow must convey this to Joan, even when it is painful; and Joan, when you feel taken for granted or are hurt, you also must communicate those sentiments to Jim, whatever the cost. A practical suggestion to make sure you communicate, you do share: Every day spend a few moments simply talking, listening to one another.

The second word is *care.* You may share or communicate perfectly, but unless you care, it makes little difference. You may know well what troubles Joan, but unless you care, Jim, you will do nothing about this. And, Joan, you too may recognize what irks Jim, but unless there is concern or care in your heart, you will have no desire to improve the situation.

Care is a synonym for love. And love entails giving. Ask your parents. They will, I am sure, tell you that marriage is a give-take, a giving-receiving relationship and that there is in it more giving than receiving. If you care, Joan, you will be more concerned about making him happy than in having your own way; if you love, Jim, you will be more intent upon pleasing her than in fulfilling your own desires. Care or love means unselfish giving. This is really the essence of married life. A second practical recommendation: Let the last words of each day, regardless of what has gone before, be "I love you."

Finally, be *fair*. All is bliss now, but all won't be heaven tomorrow. There will be disagreements, arguments, misunderstandings. There will be hurt feeling and perhaps harsh words. For you both are imperfect creatures who sometimes fail and aggravate others. These differences can either spoil and destroy your love or strengthen and deepen it. If you quickly reconcile, if you swiftly heal wounds, then your love will plunge to a new level and your joy increase. But if you allow these conflicts to continue, the wounds to fester, then misery in marriage will be your companion and marital ruin your destiny. My third bit of advice: Always make up before you fall asleep. "Never let the sun go down on your anger."

Even if you share, care, and are fair, you will still not find perfect happiness. No one has that in this life. But I think all of us here can assure you of as much joy as God gives men in our world. And you, Jim and Joan, can be certain that the Lord will stand next to you always and give you his support whenever it is needed. He is present in the sacrament you are now going to receive and he promises to be with you all the days of your life.

Chapter 4

A CHANGE OF HEART AND PEACE

In an earlier chapter, I shared with readers a critical letter from an elderly lady who assured me of her prayers, but rejected my proposal for confessional rooms or face-to-face discussion between a sympathetic priest and a troubled penitent. A later article examined the devotional use of this sacrament and concluded with a "sample confession of a housewife." Excerpted from Father John E. Corrigan's excellent little pamphlet, "Bless Me, Father," the illustration attempted to show how an honest, positive examination of conscience and telling of sins could help individuals in the growth process.

> My last confession was two weeks ago. I am a housewife and the mother of two small children. My resolution for the last few months has been to curb my tendency to nag my husband and be more cheerful with him. I think I did better during this period.
>
> I have incurred unnecessary debts and have managed the home finances poorly and selfishly.

> I learned last week that I am pregnant, and I have been depressed and felt resentful because it was unexpected. I think I have overcome these feelings now.
>
> I am only gradually adjusting to our new neighborhood. I find it hard to meet people and I have been lacking in friendliness with my new neighbors.
>
> My lenten resolution to read the New Testament every day has suffered because of the company we had last week. I'll begin again.[1]

Soon after the column's appearance I received a letter which duplicated this hypothetical housewife's confession and then added, "In the interest of justice and fair play, could you not also have published a 'sample confession of a husband' such as the following:"

> My last confession was two weeks ago. I am a husband and the father of two small children. My resolution for the past few months has been to curb my tendency to punish my wife by walking around every day with a "long face."
>
> I often stop on my way home from work to have a few drinks; consequently, I am often late for supper. This understandably upsets my wife—as it would any woman—but when she attempts to discuss it, I maintain a stubborn and sullen silence.
>
> I learned last week that my wife is pregnant again. God forgive me! I yelled at her, as though it were her fault instead of mine. I continually force myself on her, insisting that she satisfy my sexual cravings whenever I demand it. I sense that some nights she is "bone-tired" but I pretend not to notice. After all, I know my "rights."
>
> I think I have broken my wife's spirit. Forgive me, God. Forgive me. Forgive me. I fear it will be a long time before I can earn her forgiveness. . . .

We would like to hope that growth-oriented devotional confessions like these are on the increase. But that, apparently, is not the case. Contemporary Roman Catholics may indeed have moved away from fear-ridden, tension-filled use of this sacrament, but it seems many do so simply by avoiding the "box" entirely. At least priests generally sense a notable decrease in the number of confessions and that observation has been confirmed by a recent nationwide survey.

The newly formed Federation of Diocesan Liturgical Commissions submitted in April 1970 to liturgical committees of the country a questionnaire on the state of penance in the United States. Sixty-two responded. In their reply, forty-eight indicated there was a notable decrease in confessions, ten others affirmed the decline but with reservations, one saw little diminution, three had no answer.[2]

A supplementary survey of the clergy taken in a Midwest diocese fleshed out parts of this Federation questionnaire and offered a few reasons for the general trend. First of all, priests pointed to abbreviated hours for confessions, shorter waiting lines, and longer intervals between penitents as proof of the near universal decline in use of the sacrament. The following catalogue of remarks summarizes respondents' attempts to explain the phenomenon: Priests tell them not to go so often; a better understanding of sin and guilt; loss of a sense of sin; the new theology; people see no need for confession or look upon it as not very important; confession in the Church; belief that the penitential rite in Mass replaces confession; persons are less legalistic today and are changing their customs; an overall apathy toward religious matters; reaction to the earlier automatic approach in confession; poorly trained preachers and confessors; the impersonal box and lack of personal contact; emphasis on individual responsibility; need for fresh look at the hours of confessions; the neglect of preaching on the subject; and failure to meet needs of the people.[3]

What has happened to confession? Does it have a future? Has this practice proved irrelevant and passed its period of usefulness? Will we soon link confession with the rosary, Friday abstinence, novenas, medals — relics of a previous era?

I, for one, don't think so. We are not suddenly a sinless people. Men still fail, feel guilt, seek peace and forgiveness. Many turn to psychiatrists for help, a few seek relief in suicide, others unburden their hearts to a friend and confidant. Persons today perhaps more than ever ponder past mistakes, desperately wish to leave behind them their less than noble selves and move on to a fresh and better future. However, if the results of these surveys are accurate, Roman Catholics turn less and less to priests and the sacrament of penance for help in this conversion process. I hope in the present chapter to explore ways in which that regrettable trend can be reversed. I will touch on sin, repentance and the Eucharist, then look into communal penance services, and finally suggest some methods for capitalizing on the inherent potential of auricular confession.

A. Conversion and the Eucharist

The Graduate Program in Liturgical Studies at Notre Dame sponsored a conference in June 1970 on "The Liturgy of Christian Penance." Father Aidan Kavanagh, director of both the program and the conference, entitled his keynote address, "The Purpose of Christian Penance." In the lecture, this scholar argued that the matrix of Christian penance is conversion; and its purpose, communion.

Conversion, for Kavanagh, is the painful, total wrenching of a person's life style, the utter abandonment of a previous path with a consequent full acceptance of the gospel message. This metanoia or change or *conversion* comes first and foremost with baptism. We have seen in an earlier chapter the notion of death, burial, and resurrection with Christ through its saving waters. However, important and lasting as rebirth in water and the Spirit may be, the conversion required for true Christians only begins in baptism; it must continue afterwards until our individual deaths and until the kingdom in its fullness arrives. We must, as Jesus and Paul said, die daily to sin and live for God.[4]

Our fidelity to this commitment varies, unfortunately. We waver because of weakness, discouragement, malice, pressure, passion, temptation. We stumble and fall, we are less ready at some moments than at others to accept the cross and the death to selfishness which goes with it. Later we regret this regression, this lack of faithfulness to the Lord. We turn to Christ once more, promise to set sin aside, vow to follow his words and example. These postbaptismal conversions don't always occur in the confessional or even conclude there. But they represent the essence of Christian penance, a change of heart, a renewal of the inner person, a metanoia.

We find in the New Testament abundant references to these notions of repentance and pardon, conversion and faith, penance and new life.[5] But texts of the Bible also indicate this as an ongoing struggle, a battle which never ends. Paul, in his farewell address, warned the elders at Ephesus: "So be on your guard, remembering how night and day for three years I never failed to keep you right, shedding tears over each one of you."[6] This scriptural emphasis on personal effort or human metanoia must always, however, be weighed in terms of an equally rich biblical testimony about the Father's unceasing love for man. It is God who initiates the conversion process. He touches the person's heart, he moves him to repent, he forgives, he waits for the prodigal son to return, he rejoices over the finding of a lost sheep.

In developing any liturgy of Christian penance, whether for communal services or auricular confessions, the priest and worship committee need to incorporate within them some words from Scripture which speak of God's desire to hear, accept, forgive, his wish that repentant men go in peace. A few of the more familiar quotations quickly come to mind: Luke 15 (the lost sheep and the lost drachma, the prodigal son), Luke 19:1-10 (Zacchaeus), Matthew 9:1-13 (Jesus' cure of a paralytic and his eating with sinners), Luke 7:36-50 (the woman who anointed Christ, commonly thought of as Mary Magdalene), John 8:1-11 (the adulterous woman), John 20:19-23 ("Receive the Holy Spirit. For those whose sins you forgive. . . ."). A reflective reading of one or several such texts by a lector in the public penance rite or by a penitent before his confession should instill hope and confidence in the heart of a person who has wandered away and now wishes to come home.

This brings us to the second essential notion in penance, *communion*. The sinner has cut himself off from God, from Jesus, from the Christian community. Conversion means he wishes to be reconciled, to be accepted, to be reunited with his God, his Savior, his Church. An oft-quoted passage from the conciliar text on the Church outlines the process:

> Those who approach the sacrament of penance obtain par-
> don from the mercy of God for offenses committed against
> Him. They are at the same time reconciled with the
> Church, which they have wounded by their sins, and which
> by charity, example, and prayer seeks their conversion.[7]

Jesus has fashioned himself a People, a living body of persons bound together by common beliefs and mutual love. Every sin after baptism weakens the healthiness of that Mystical Body; slight ones disrupt an individual's bond with his brother Christians, serious ones break the contact entirely. Since the Church primarily happens or becomes when Christians assemble around an altar for the Eucharist, it follows that total exclusion from the Church means above all separation from the eucharistic table and, conversely, full reconciliation with the Church means primarily restoration to the community in the context of a Mass.

We have a parallel to this in everyday living. A misbehaving child at the evening meal will first be warned by the parents, then threatened with loss of dessert, and finally, as a last resort, sent upstairs before dinner ends. His actions have disrupted the community, broken the bond of familial love and peace. He must leave, therefore, until he changes his attitude and remain alone in his room until he is willing to reform. When the conversion comes, however, parents, brothers, sisters welcome him (hopefully) back with open arms; all is forgiven; the family rejoices; the community feels at one again.[8]

This brings us to the question of the Eucharist's power to remit sins. Father John Quinn's article in *Worship*, "The Lord's Supper and Forgiveness of Sin," discusses the issue at length. His introduction places the matter in perspective.

> At present, baptism and penance have an exclusive role as
> the sacraments of pardon. Baptism removes original sin and
> with confirmation and the eucharist initiates one into the
> Christian life; it is also the basis for receiving the sacrament
> of penance. But penance is considered the sacrament of
> pardon *par excellence* because it purifies the Christian for
> the reception of communion. Yet baptism has a continuing
> effect of pardon and the eucharist is the perfection of the

remission of sins because the cross, the mystery of reconciliation, is present in it alone. For centuries the church
lived on these truths, allowing the sacrament of penance its
extraordinary role. Since the Middle Ages the remission of
sins conferred by the eucharist has suffered almost complete neglect.[9]

Quinn notes the Church's official teaching on different occasions (the Council of Trent, the Instruction on Eucharistic
Worship of 1967) with regard to the Eucharist's purifying effects.
He also traces evidences of this belief in Jewish, New Testament, and liturgical sources. We might in passing observe how
some of our current prayers at Mass presuppose this power of
the eucharistic celebration to forgive sins.

O Lord, may the reception of your blessed sacrament
cleanse us from sin and make us one. (Postcommunion,
Ninth Sunday after Pentecost)

O Lord, look with mercy upon the offerings we are placing upon your altar. May they win pardon for our sins and
give glory to your name. (Prayer over the Gifts, Twelfth
Sunday after Pentecost)

May the reception of this sacrament bring us life, O
Lord, and win for us your pardon and protection. (Postcommunion, Twelfth Sunday after Pentecost)

O Lord, look with favor upon your people and their gifts.
Let this offering move you to compassion, and grant us forgiveness for our sins and a speedy answer to our prayers.
(Prayer over the Gifts, Thirteenth Sunday after Pentecost)[10]

Father Quinn concludes his study with this summary:

The doctrine of remission of sins conferred by the eucharist
has had a long and varied history of use and neglect in the
church. Granted that the forgiveness of sins is not the chief
object of the eucharist and that no one wants a return to the
days when the mass was over-emphasized as a sacrifice of
propitiation for sin, Christ made the forgiveness of sins an

essential dimension of it. The eucharist must of course be approached with purity of intention. A penitential act which is part of the eucharist can help to achieve it. But we should not want a penitential preparation at the beginning which would convey the idea of achieving forgiveness of sins as something separate from the eucharist itself, which would be simply joy and praise, admiration and thanksgiving.[11]

The penitential service at the beginning of Mass, the Our Father, the sign of peace are all ritualistic actions with conciliatory overtones and an implication of God's forgiveness for sin. However, to judge any of these as sacramental absolution at whatever point in Mass they come, would, as Quinn asserts, unnecessarily obscure and duplicate the effect of the sacrifice-meal.

The structures of the two sacraments are different. Perhaps penance might be likened to the shepherd seeking the lost sheep and to the prodigal son returning home. But the eucharist is the father celebrating with his son the meal of reconciliation.[12]

A further objection arises concerning the suggestion sometimes made that the revised Order of Mass does or ought to include sacramental absolution, especially in the introductory penitential rite. We know that lesser sins can be forgiven in numerous ways—by a kind deed, a prayer, a blessing. The prayer for forgiveness terminating the penance service in eucharistic celebrations obviously fits into that category and holds the power to remit venial moral failures. But would it be wise, pastorally speaking, to make this simple gesture, with little preparation, adequate for remission of serious sins and reconciliation of major offenders? Is everyone in the congregation on a Sunday morning so disposed for such an absolution? Could this not lead to mere formalism and mechanical repetition? Would we not then be truly open to the older criticism that Catholics sin easily and are forgiven even more easily? Does this not almost eliminate personal responsibility for our actions? Is not conversion involving a major change of heart more than a few seconds of silence, a brief common prayer, and a phrase by some priest? The penitential rite helps in the total conversion process, prepares us more perfectly for the Eucharist, and complements the sacrament of penance. But in my opinion it neither does nor should replace auricular confession or communal penance services.

B. Communal Penance Services

The Council Fathers directed in the reform of the sacred liturgy that "whenever rites, according to their specific nature, make provision for communal celebration involving the presence and active participation of the faithful, this way of celebrating them is to be preferred, as far as possible, to a celebration that is individual and quasi-private."[13] The average Roman Catholic, however, probably does not consider confession and the sacrament of penance in terms of a public service or a communal celebration. He thinks of dark, secret, anonymous confessional "boxes," and of the eternal seal which closes a priest's lips and keeps him silent about sins mentioned by anxious penitents. For that person, penance is something very private, very personal, very individualistic.

In some ways, of course, this approach should not be questioned. Every man ultimately must stand alone before God, each person bears responsibility for his own decisions, his own virtues, his own failures. In addition, I know of few liturgists or theologians who would opt for a public recitation of intimate, specific sins. We need to be open persons and shake some of our false inhibitions or artificial defenses, but this, it seems to me, hardly means a total unveiling of our inner selves to all. Sin, penance, forgiveness, then, do legitimately possess certain personal, private characteristics. Any reform or development of the liturgy must respect that point.

On the other hand, to quote a new paperback on confession, "At the bottom of it all: Life is social, love is social, sin is social."[14] So, too, mercy and reconciliation are social. As we discussed earlier, sin cuts us off from the community of believers and adversely affects the Church's well-being. Consequently, forgiveness presumes some type of restoration to and through the Church. Communal penance services seek to stress these concepts—the social nature of sin, the community's concern, forgiveness and acceptance of a repentant sinner, God's constant love for a straying member of his flock, and the Lord's unceasing desire that a profligate come to his senses.

First of all, we should explore a bit more fully the social nature of sin. Father Corrigan in an address, "Penance: A Service to the Community," at the 1966 North American Liturgical Week in Houston traced through biblical texts and contemporary experience the idea of sin as an offense not only against God, but also against the whole Church and all mankind.[15] Adam and Eve, Cain, Solomon, David—the sins of each spread in their effects far beyond the individuals who committed them. St. Paul in the fifth chapter to the Romans talks of mankind's solidarity in sin and of our corresponding union in righteousness or deliverance from sin. Corrigan cites some concrete modern instances in which a sin is not simply "my sin," but a transgression which affects many others.

> Take the divisions within Christianity itself. Have not the sixteenth-century sins of pride, stubbornness, and self-righteousness evolved into the quarrelsome splintering of the past few centuries? However righteous the zeal which fed the enmity, many of us recognize today that the whole Christian body suffered severe injury.
>
> Sin is like a stone thrown into the pond of the universe. President Kennedy's death at the hands of an assassin occasioned another equally senseless act of murder, the killing of the assassin.
>
> Who is not aware of the far-reaching consequences of the sin of war? For war is not only an evil on the battlefield but spreads its poison throughout the world. Widows and fatherless children are obvious results. Less apparent are the anxieties, the mental illnesses, the marital infidelities, the insecurity of children, and the temptation of avarice that mistakes war for a boon to business.
>
> Another deeply rooted source of sin is the racial attitudes among the Christians in our big cities which beget active prejudice, discrimination, and violence.

All of us are aware of young adults who find it almost impossible to prepare properly for marriage because of the "everyone-does-it" philosophy.[16]

The Bishops of Holland in 1965 issued a pastoral letter on the public celebration of penance. The following paragraph is pertinent to our discussion:

It is also advisable that the priest with care of souls make use of the celebration of public penance to awaken in the faithful an ever increasing awareness of the social and ecclesial dimensions of human guilt. In this way they may help to form their conscience with greater depth and make them understand more fully how each one of us, personally and collectively, is responsible for every existing sin in the human community.[17]

The other purposes of these community penance celebrations—an awareness of God's mercy and of reconciliation through the Church—are brought out in the rite itself. A liturgy of the Word with appropriate scriptural readings and accompanying homily makes our merciful Lord present as he addresses us through the inspired text. Prayers and actions (e.g., a commonly recited penance, prayers while individuals confess in private, the sign of peace) underscore a congregation's concern for each individual and the community's embrace of a repentant sinner as he rejoins the assembly of believing Christians.

In 1969 the Liturgical Commission for the Madison diocese issued a document, "The Sacrament of Reconciliation," which contained guidelines for a communal penance service. As it mentions, however, these were suggestions only, with details to be determined by the worship committee which prepares the specific celebration. It will be for that group to determine how a given ceremony can best express the social dimension of sin, the Father's never-ending mercy, and the community's acceptance of the penitent person. The Madison outline which we reproduce below should prove helpful as a starting point in this planning process.

A Communal Penitential Service should include the following elements: entrance music and opening prayer by a priest, scriptural reading(s), homily, lay people's response, confession, absolution, penance, recessional.

The following is a more detailed explanation of the above elements, but need not be considered absolute. Creativity and flexibility in planning for the penitential service is encouraged.

A. Entrance Music and Opening Prayer by a Priest.
   1. Entrance of priest and lay readers.
   2. Music — chant or sing a song of repentance or joy at the forgiveness of God.
   3. Prayer — by a priest with short meditation period.

B. Scriptural Reading(s).
   The use of the Word of God in both Old and New Testament emphasizes that the Sacrament of Penance is not only to forgive but leads the man of faith to a greater spiritual maturity and complies with a recommendation from Vatican Council II to utilize Scripture. The scriptural reading(s) can point out what sinfulness is in the eyes of God; it can point out the obligations of the individual to the ecclesial community, illustrate the mercy of God or may dwell upon special problems facing the community.

C. Homily.
   The homily should be a *short* but instructive period of moral guidance.
   The following themes are recommended for the initial penitential services:
   1. Sin means renouncing one's whole basic attitude of confidence in God.
   2. Penance is a re-presenting, not just evoking, but really making present again — the moment in history when Jesus sought pardon for the human nature which He shared with us. Through this Sacrament we share in that setting foot on the road of reconciling man to God which Jesus took before us and we continue the renewal originally experienced in baptism.
   3. The Sacrament of Penance has the elements of sor-

row for offending God and the community, and reconciliation to both is essential.

D. Lay People's Response.
1. Period of personal reflection.
2. Prayers of Petition—The prayers should have a positive expression, e.g., 'For the times we have been hypocritical, forgive me, O God, and my brothers.'
3. Act of Sorrow.
4. Handshake of Reconciliation among penitents themselves. This period need not be solemn, indeed, there is much joy in the knowledge of the return to the community of one who had rejected it and God.

E. Confession.
At this point of the liturgy an opportunity should be provided for each individual penitent to meet the priest in the setting in which he is comfortable, that is, standing and speaking to the priest, kneeling and confessing in the open or the use of the confessional, observing the norms prescribed by Canon Law and moral theology. Grave faults must be mentioned in number and in kind. The period of guidance during this type of liturgy is limited and the priest is encouraged to meet in private with the penitent if serious moral or psychological problems are encountered.

F. Absolution and Penance.
1. Absolution—The priests in unison may confer absolution on the reassembled community or it may be given in private as each confesses.
2. Penance—It is encouraged to give the penance collectively to the community in that it again stresses ecclesiality.

G. Recessional—Song of Joy.[18]

The committee which seeks additional help in detailing communal penance services will find suggestions for readings, prayers, group examinations of conscience, etc., available in several recent publications.[19] One, in particular, deserves special mention: *Healing and Forgiveness*, a $1.35 paperback subtitled, "A New Penitential," published by the World Library of Sacred Music.[20]

C. Private Auricular Confession

A priest in the Archdiocese of San Francisco who has conducted group penitential services finds that these do not replace, but rather, complement private confessions. Those who have participated in such services seem to confess with a greater understanding of the sacrament, a deeper appreciation of sin and forgiveness, a better growth-centered attitude toward auricular confession. In brief, according to the Bay Area liturgist, these communal celebrations seem to enhance the quality of private penance experiences, even may, although this has not yet been verified, increase their frequency.

Whatever the case, few would debate the need for some *aggiornamento* in the practices surrounding private auricular confession. My critic of eighty years in Chapter Thirteen finds no difficulty in dark, cramped "boxes" or with the impersonalism which often surrounds the administration of this sacrament. Many others, however, do reject the in-and-out, three Our Fathers and three Hail Marys, no words of advice, the grocery list of sins, the same failures month after month approach. True, as the good lady mentions, faith is all essential. Conversion happens in *my* heart, not the confessor's. I should be mature enough as a person and strong enough in my beliefs to pass over the obstacles of an uncomfortable setting, an insensitive priest, a legalistic religious education and concentrate on the essentials — sin, conversion, forgiveness, peace. But not all of us are that mature or that strong. The celebrations of penance, like those of the Eucharist, should be humanly attractive experiences. Good ones nourish and strengthen our faith; poor ones weaken and destroy it. In the following pages I would like to suggest a few ways in which we can improve our contemporary celebrations of confession and make them good ones, personal encounters with the saving Lord in which he moves us to repent, accepts our change of heart, forgives our sins, motivates us to improve, and sends us away in peace.[21]

We begin with something very neutral — the physical setting and, in particular, our confessional "boxes." The one I sit in each Saturday afternoon epitomizes all that is bad about them. It has noisy wooden doors for confessor and penitent, pitch-black interiors, cramped spacing, poor ventilation, sound-through acoustics. The church was constructed about a decade ago and the architect no doubt simply followed patterns traditional at the time. But one hardly would see this confessional as an ideal location for a warm, joyful, peace-giving dialogue with Christ, the merciful Savior.

The weakness of that absolutely dark, totally impersonal, and utterly anonymous procedure perhaps could be illustrated by an incident from Noah Gordon's novel, *The Rabbi*, a book I have used frequently in my writings and lectures for young people. Michael Kind, the rabbi and central character, is on his second date with Leslie Rawlings, the daughter of a Congregationalist minister who later will become Kind's wife. She "confesses" to him an affair of the previous summer. The rabbi tries to halt this personal unburdening, but Leslie insists and gives the reason why:

> "Yes, don't you see, I haven't been able to tell anybody, but this is so safe. This is practically made to order. You're a rabbi and I'm a . . . a *shickseh*, and we'll probably never see each other again. It's even better than if I were a Catholic telling it to a priest hidden behind a screen in a confessional, because I *know* the kind of person you are."[22]

I am not arguing here for face-to-face confessions only or all the time; this would be intolerant liturgical liberalism, a narrowing of choices for penitents. Some individuals do not want to and never will confess in such fashion. But others would be happier at least recognizing the priest's image, if not sitting in a chair opposite him. In the construction of new churches or the renovation of old ones, we should design confessional boxes or, and preferably, rooms to give people the maximum number of options and to surround them with an atmosphere which communicates that mercy and joy proper to the sacrament of penance.

The Baton Rouge Cathedral illustrates well what can be done in this regard when a church is restored for use with the revised liturgy. A two-for-one box (a person on either side of the confessor so he will not lose precious seconds while one leaves and another enters) was removed and replaced with a small room. The confessor sits in an amply lighted section behind a partition which runs three-fourths of the width of the room. The penitent enters and has the option of kneeling in anonymity behind a screen (but one which reveals the features of the priest's head and shoulders) or of walking around the wall, taking the chair provided, and facing the confessor. A third possibility, sitting on the opposite side of the partition from the priest, would help the elderly and the crippled, or those who wish to discuss matters at length with the confessor, but prefer to remain unknown or unseen.

Those responsible for the decoration of these confessionals could do much to establish an appropriate atmosphere through carpeting, soft, but adequate lighting, pleasant colors, and artistic designs which convey God's love for men in the past and his merciful dealings with them at the present in this sacrament. In such an arrangement both penitent and confessor can talk, not whisper, and neither need fear the conversation will be overheard by a person kneeling in discomfort and impatience on the other side.

A church near Baltimore has taken a different path to supply parishioners with these options. A room in the rectory is reserved for open confessions with priests rotating on Saturdays between more typical confessionals in the church proper and this space set aside in the parish house. The Sunday bulletin specifies who will hear and where and at what hours. This procedure does eliminate the awkwardness of long delays for those who wish to confess rather simply and yet must wait for the penitent in need of a lengthy interchange with his or her confessor.

The crux of the matter, however, rests not in the redesign of confessional boxes but in the reorientation of human hearts. Confession will truly die as a means of growth for concerned Christians and a way toward peace for troubled sinners unless some kind of catechetical program for the young and the old unveils the real possibilities of this sacrament. If you stopped almost any priest in the nation and asked him about confessions, he probably would say they are down, they are dying, no one goes anymore. Members of religious committees no doubt would respond in a similar vein. A partner of mine on the handball court—educated in Catholic schools from elementary grades through the graduate level, extremely conscientious about his religious duties and aware of his spiritual responsibilities as a father—admits he goes much less often to confession. Furthermore, his children, despite parochial school formation, rarely walk up the street to church on a Saturday afternoon and confess their sins. This phenomenon, as we documented earlier, appears rather general. Some would see it as progress, others wring their hands about the decline in faith among Catholics they purport it reflects, and still others feel confused about the entire situation.

What, however, seems even clearer is the nearly complete absence of constructive catechesis on penance. I get the impression we have all dropped the subject like a hot potato, have walked away from a perplexing issue, and have preferred to say nothing at home or in school on the matter. Perhaps this trend merely mirrors the hesitation on everyone's part today to teach religion during the present era of controversy or confusion. In Minnesota, a six-diocese survey reported that 47 percent of the high school religion teachers would not teach this subject at all in the 1970-71 academic year.[23] If those figures are accurate concerning the subject of religion in general, then we certainly can assume they hold true to an even greater degree for a specific area like confession or penance.

Such a formational program, and I obviously think one is urgently needed, must begin with the true nature of sin, conversion, and forgiveness. We have lightly touched on these concerns in the previous pages. With regard to confession, it should then very concretely show children (and adults) how to examine their consciences both on a daily basis and in preparation for confession. Unfortunately, suitable writings in this realm are few in number. We have many leaflets, pamphlets, even books on the subject; but they tend to concentrate on narrow and negative points—the number of times, the kind and seriousness of a sin.

That approach often misses the mark, fails to dig down deep or get at the sinner's attitude and, more significantly, his resolutions for tomorrow. Similarly, these manuals frequently, although not intentionally, minimize the divine content of confession and exaggerate the human element.

There are a few publications, however, which could be helpful. Corrigan's little pamphlet, by offering sample confessions for different classes of people, indirectly teaches how one should examine his conscience.[24] Father Foley's paperback contains an appendix giving "Examples of Brief Confessions of Sinfulness." These twenty-plus illustrations similarly, by way of indirection, pose questions a person could and ought to ask himself at the end of a day or before approaching the sacrament of penance.[25] *The Book of Catholic Worship* published in 1966 by the Liturgical Conference includes a section on penance and, in it, a lengthy treatise on the examination of conscience. A host of questions in separate sections have been designed to lead both adults and children into serious and probing self-inquiries. The following topical headings reflect the thoroughness of this text. "What kind of an employee am I? What kind of an employer am I? As a professional person do I make an honest effort to live up to the ideals of my profession? What kind of a husband am I? What kind of a wife am I? As a single person, am I careful to avoid selfishness? Do I take a responsible part in the political affairs of my city, state and nation? Do I live as a member of my parish family? Am I aware of the social implications of my Christian life?" A reader will find many pointed, specific questions under each of those general categories. These from the final question concerning social implications seem representative.

> Do I avoid and condemn any form of racial prejudice, wherever and however it might be practiced? Do I try to eliminate any form of prejudice in myself, and do I speak out against it whenever I encounter it? What have I done to remove this evil from the community in which I live? How have I supported those who are working to remove it from the state and national level?

What have I done for people who are poorer than I am? Do I encourage and support efforts to allow every member of society to live a decent life? Have I helped to make happier the lives of the sick, the old, or those in prision?

Do I realize what human rights are and do I work to make them realities in every life? Through gossip or by other means do I destroy the good name of another? Do I uphold by word and deed the right of every person to live where he wishes? Do I ridicule those who exercise their right to protest?

Do I work for peace? Am I willing to involve myself in efforts to find peaceful solutions to neighborhood, community and state problems? Do I do what I can to promote international peace? Do I encourage my representatives to seek every possibility for achieving genuine peace in the world? Do I recognize that no nation, religion, or social system claims a monopoly on all truth?

Do I allow a proper love of country to turn into a narrow nationalism, or do I actively recognize the brotherhood of all men? Do I support and encourage efforts to assist underdeveloped nations, to give all men a chance to help themselves? Am I willing to make sacrifices to see that this is done?[26]

The way in which a penitent actually relates his sins to the priest will naturally depend in great measure upon the kind of progress he has made in examining his conscience. Those fictional examples in the beginning of this chapter presuppose a husband who has taken a hard look at his own heart or a wife who is really concerned about personal growth. Confessions like these are painful and embarrassing experiences. To run through a list of rather abstract universal sins—"I was uncharitable, negligent in my duties, impatient"—takes some courage; to speak about them in concrete, particular terms—"I spread a rumor about my next-door neighbor because I wanted to get some attention during a conversation with several others, I failed to speak up in defense of someone who was being falsely attacked for fear it would hurt my future in the business, I lost my temper with my son and hurt his feelings when he accidentally spilled something"—requires much more. The healing power of the latter type of confession far exceeds, I think, that of the former, quite impersonal relation of sins.

In a word, we do not espouse a nerve-wracking, computer-like enumeration of *all* our minor faults. We recommend, instead, taking a few failings which truly bother us, which we honestly regret, and speaking of them in such fashion that it hurts us. The future may see us fall back into the same habits and repeat former sins—the spirit is willing, but the weakness of the flesh often prevails. However, confessions which take something out of us very likely will push us to put something into improvement. The chance of mechanical formalism is less; the possibility of conversion and growth, much greater.

For better and for worse, a priest's importance in the sacrament of penance parallels the significance of his function in eucharistic celebrations and other liturgical ceremonies. If he says the correct words, does the right thing, possesses the proper power and intention, God works through him and communicates grace to the penitent. But the measure of this grace, the extent of confession's fruitfulness often is diminished or increased by the celebrant's plus or minus qualities. Harsh, insensitive words, an abrupt cutting off of the person or slamming of the slide, the routine utterance of advice and imposition of penance, a silent or bored or speedy recitation of absolution can send offended individuals away never to return or leave sincere Catholics discouraged, disillusioned, distressed. On the other hand, the warm, understanding, patient confessor, ready to listen and anxious to help, dismisses the once burdened, now relieved; once troubled, now peaceful; once downcast, now uplifted with renewed determination for the future struggle against the world, the flesh, and the devil.

Imaginative penances agreed upon by the alert priest and willing penitent may add a final touch to this conversion process. A penance linked with the sin confessed and oriented toward the contrary virtue can give guilt-ridden persons a sense of "making up" for their failure and aid them in moving forward along the better path. For example, an unfaithful partner might promise in some way to compensate for his lack of loyalty (take her out for dinner, do something she enjoys); one who has erred with his tongue might promise to say something good about the person injured; an intemperate individual might promise to make an act of personal self-denial.

All of these steps are possible now without waiting for revisions in the liturgical celebration of this sacrament. At the same time, a reform in the texts and in the procedures should further increase the attractiveness of penance for contemporary man. What can we expect from the Congregation for Divine Worship? Probably elements of this nature: a better welcome or blessing ceremony, freedom to develop more personal avowals of sinfulness, suggested constructive penances, possible imposition of hands or a similar external sign which indicates restoration and reconciliation, an absolution formula (perhaps a variety of them) which more clearly expresses a notion of return to the integrity of the Christian community, speaks about the action of the Holy Spirit in this healing and forgiveness process, and refers directly to Christ's forgiveness.[27]

With regard to the last item, these two conjectured texts illustrate future possibilities, the one a deprecatory prayer form and the other a declarative expression of forgiveness.

"Our Lord Jesus Christ reconciled the world to his Father. May he reconcile you through my ministry to his Church and to himself."

"Our Lord Jesus Christ has forgiven you through my ministry by his Spirit."[28]

Communal penance services and private auricular confessions remain only means to an end, albeit valuable and indispensable means. The goal in view is a true conversion of heart and the deep peace which flows from reconciliation with God and with his people.

Chapter 5

ON DYING, DEATH, AND RISING

The central doctrine which dominates documents of Vatican II and postconciliar reforms is the paschal mystery of Jesus' dying, rising, coming again. The Constitution on the Sacred Liturgy teaches that our Lord instituted the Last Supper on Holy Thursday precisely as a paschal banquet to perpetuate his life-giving sacrifice.

> At the Last Supper, on the night when He was betrayed, our Savior instituted the Eucharistic Sacrifice of His Body and Blood. He did this in order to perpetuate the sacrifice of the Cross throughout the centuries until He should come again, and so to entrust to His beloved spouse, the Church, a memorial of His death and resurrection: a sacrament of love, a sign of unity, a bond of charity, a paschal banquet in which Christ is consumed, the mind is filled with grace, and a pledge of future glory is given to us.[1]

What Christ initiated and commanded, the Church has faithfully observed from its beginning until the present moment. The same decree notes:

> From that time onward the Church has never failed to come together to celebrate the paschal mystery: reading "in all the scriptures the things referring to himself" (Luke 24:27), celebrating the Eucharist in which "the victory and triumph of his death are again made present," and at the same time giving thanks "to God for his unspeakable gift" (2 Cor. 9:15) in Christ Jesus, "to the praise of his glory" (Eph. 1:12), through the power of the Holy Spirit.[2]

Every Mass, then, recalls and makes present this Easter triumph, but the Sunday eucharistic celebration does so in a very special, tradition-rich way. The revised Church calendar comments:

> The Church celebrates the paschal mystery on the first day of the week, known as the Lord's Day or Sunday. This follows a tradition handed down from the Apostles, which took its origin from the day of Christ's resurrection. Thus Sunday should be considered "the original feast day."[3]

Finally, Easter and the fifty days which follow until Pentecost uniquely commemorate this mystery we celebrate at every Eucharist and on each Sunday.

> Christ redeemed mankind and gave perfect glory to God principally through his paschal mystery: by dying he destroyed our death and by rising he restored our life. The Easter triduum of the passion and resurrection of Christ is thus the culmination of the entire liturgical year. What Sunday is to the week, the solemnity of Easter is to the liturgical year.[4]
>
> The fifty days between Easter Sunday and Pentecost are celebrated as one feast day, sometimes called "the great Sunday."[5]

These truths should be more evident to Roman Catholics with the recent introduction of new Eucharistic Prayers. Acclamations which follow the institution narrative express our belief in this paschal mystery (e.g., "Dying you destroyed our death, rising you restored our life. Lord Jesus, come in glory."[6]) So, too, the memorial prayers or offering at that point of the Mass explicitly speak of this Easter concept. Eucharistic Prayer III offers a good illustration.

> Father, calling to mind the death your Son endured
> for our salvation,
> his glorious resurrection and ascension into heaven,
> and ready to greet him when he comes again,
> we offer you in thanksgiving this holy and living
> sacrifice.[7]

Our share in Christ's paschal mystery begins with baptism, continues, hopefully, through a life of faith and love, and culminates when we die, then rise to the fullness of total union with Jesus, his Father, and the Holy Spirit. It remains for me in this book to treat, liturgically and pastorally, those final moments of sickness, dying, death, and burial. Here the Church concentrates once more in her worship on the paschal mystery since it is this which gives the ailing Christian or anxious family hope for eternal life.

A. Anointing of the Sick

During his life on earth, Jesus toured towns and villages, "curing all kinds of diseases and sickness."[8] Later he gave his apostles "power and authority over all devils and to cure diseases, and he sent them out to proclaim the kingdom of God and to heal."[9] In response to this command the Twelve "set off to preach repentance; and they cast out many devils, and anointed many sick people with oil and cured them."[10]

What was intimated in St. Mark as a sacrament for the anointing of the sick becomes recommended, even promulgated, by the classic text of St. James.

> If one of you is ill, he should send for the elders of the
> church, and they must anoint him with oil in the name of
> the Lord and pray over him. The prayer of faith will save

the sick man and the Lord will raise him up again; and if he has committed any sins, he will be forgiven. So confess your sins to one another, and pray for one another, and this will cure you; the heartfelt prayer of a good man works very powerfully.[11]

For the first nine Christian centuries the specific purpose of this sacrament was judged to be the physical healing of a sick person, although men naturally felt it also would bring about an overall spiritual improvement in the infirm. Recovery from the illness, a return to one's duties, restoration to active participation in the Eucharist were seen as the proper effects of that anointing. By the twelfth century, however, emphasis had shifted, with the sacrament administered after Viaticum and when death seemed imminent. It became a sacrament for the departing—extreme unction, the last anointing, the final sacrament. Its goal was to prepare the soul for immediate entrance into heaven and removal of venial, even mortal, sins was the means by which extreme unction accomplished this end.

With the Council of Trent we catch beginnings of a reform, a recognition once again that anointing of the sick can effect a physical cure of the body as well as a moral cleansing of the soul. The "danger of death" condition still prevailed, but official doctrine embraced a wider, more biblically oriented interpretation of the sacrament. The Code of Canon Law early in this century insisted that recipients possess the use of reason (thus the anointing could not be used simply for healing purposes), but it defined more liberally the phrase "danger of death from illness or old age." That approach, practically speaking, meant an acknowledgment of the physically curative power in this sacrament.

The Constitution on the Sacred Liturgy carries all of this several steps further by urging a return to the former name, "Anointing of the Sick," by stating it is "not a sacrament for those only who are at the point of death," and by directing a revival of the earlier order in which a sick person confesses, is anointed, and finally receives Viaticum.[12]

This last change envisions Viaticum as truly the "last" sacrament. The Risen Christ in his eucharistic presence is our food for the final journey, our pledge of ultimate resurrection, our bread from heaven which gives hope for eternal life. The anointing of the sick, on the contrary, gives strength to the sick person so he may bear his illness bravely and with supernatural serenity. It forgives, if necessary, his sins, and, God willing, restores or improves his health.[13]

At the present writing we do not have the finalized version of the revised Roman rite for the anointing of the sick. However, preliminary reports, the experiment at Lourdes with a communal celebration of this sacrament, and the pattern of reform in other already published liturgical books offer us some indication of what to expect.

Flexibility, of course, stands at the head of the list. The priest (working with a family or community) will have a rich selection of prayers, scriptural readings, and blessings from which to choose. The text followed at that famous French shrine includes, for example, ten Old Testament excerpts, six paschal time selections for the first reading, nineteen New Testament passages for regular usage, twenty-four gospel pericopes and assorted readings from the history of the Lord's Passion.[14] Moreover, official guidelines will undoubtedly leave much to the discretion of the national body of bishops and to the judgment of a specific celebrant.

Stress on the faith and community aspects in this celebration comes next in the order of importance. The magical, run-through-red-lights-and-get-there-at-any-cost approach of priests may, in view of this emphasis, begin to disappear. Not that we wish to discourage frequent, conscientious visitation of the sick or prompt response to emergencies, but sometimes the attitude of Catholics in these situations really would grant more efficacy to this anointing ceremony than God intended. Catechesis may, in time, lead our laity to ask for the sacrament early, when an ill individual may with strong, active, and conscious faith share in and be visibly strengthened by the service.

St. James talks about the power of faith and prayer to heal. All liturgical actions should, whenever possible, follow a communal format. Anointing is no exception. The Lourdes' experiment brings many sick people, their relatives, and friends together for the celebration of the sacrament in a eucharistic context. This anointing within Mass means mutual sharing, praying, and caring by members of the Christian community. The restored ritual will certainly provide for such common participation both in these larger settings and in the privacy of a home.

We have already discussed the reasons behind the celebration of baptism at Mass. Many of the points made then hold true for the anointing of the sick administered within a eucharistic setting. Baptism prepares us for the future when we will receive our Lord in Holy Communion. In somewhat parallel fashion, anointing, with Viaticum, leads us either to that moment when we will see Jesus in glory or back to full health when we can again join with the community at the altar for the Eucharist.

The number of anointings will be modified and the form somewhat altered. The Lourdes' rite provides for anointment with oil of the forehead and extended hands, instead of the customary practice which anoints all the senses. The reformed ritual probably will follow that innovation, and its formula during this anointing will express the sacrament's several purposes that we mentioned earlier. The so-called "form" might read something like this:

> (Priest anoints forehead) "Through this holy anointing and his most loving mercy may the Lord fill you with the grace of the Holy Spirit." All respond: "Amen." (Priest anoints hands) "And freed from every power of sin may he save you and generously refresh you." All respond: "Amen."

Revisions from Rome of the official text for anointing (as with baptism, marriage, and the other sacraments) form only a part of the thorough renewal called for by Pope John XXIII and the Council Fathers. Unless there is sound instruction of the people in liturgical matters and full use of the potential in the options available, we will have simply replaced one set of rites and rubrics with another.

The National Association of Catholic Chaplains, with secretarial headquarters in Washington, has established a base for the kind of pastoral work which can lead to deep and fruitful celebrations of this sacrament for the sick. In addition to an English translation of the Lourdes' communal service, that organization has published "Guidelines for the Visitation and Care of the Sick," a series of thirty-seven suggestions for the clergy prepared by several chaplains active in this apostolate.[15]

Moreover, one subcommittee assembled a collection of scriptural readings and prayers for the sick and dying, tested them in practice, indexed the biblical passages according to thirty-seven themes (e.g., comfort, faith, forgiveness, healing, impartiality, patience, prayer, self-destruction, suffering, trust), and arranged for their publication by a commercial firm.[16] This inexpensive pamphlet, "Fear Not I Am With You," should really become a must for every priest, every family with a member seriously ill, every hospital room. Many times the priest on his visitation feels speechless and hates to utter some trite phrase, but through fatigue or routine cannot come up with a suitable replacement. Likewise, lay friends and relatives sense an obligation to sit by the bedside and offer support, but fail to find words which express their good intentions and inner feelings. This booklet solves that difficulty. The visitor, clerical or lay, may pick it up, read a passage or two, recite one of the prayers, even, when the patient's condition permits, alternately pray with the sick person verses from a psalm. God is present in his holy Word. Reverent reading of texts supplied in this scripturally oriented book brings that special presence into the sick room. Later and alone, ill individuals able to read may take great comfort from these excerpts and find their fears allayed because Christ is truly with them.

One can hope that these various notions of the paschal mystery, resurrection, Eucharist and Sacred Scripture will be translated into practical terms through increased use of laymen for the bearing of Communion to the sick. Perhaps a majority of dioceses now employ men (and women) to assist priests in the distribution of the Eucharist at Masses or in hospitals. This writer, however, foresees a day in which we will go further and make it common practice for laity, specially deputed for the occasion, to carry on Sunday after Mass the Risen Lord to persons confined at home. A brief biblical service and homily (based on the parish liturgy) followed by Holy Communion will give the infirm a sense of sharing in the earlier celebration offered by the full community of healthy members.

Such a procedure has already begun in Belgium and Canada. The former hierarchy, in initiating this innovation, composed an "Episcopal Letter to the Sick" to be signed by a bishop, then presented by priests to the infirm as they visit them, and inform parishioners about the new practice. These two paragraphs nicely summarize the "why and how" behind this re-establishment of a very ancient tradition in the Church.

> It is very clear that only the priest can *consecrate* the bread into the Body of Christ; but from now on, your fellow Christians will be associated with him in *carrying the Eucharist*. Until now, many parishioners confined to their home could not benefit from the Eucharist except on very infrequent occasions. They were nearly always deprived of Holy Communion on Sundays and feast days. In the future, it will be possible for you to receive Communion more frequently — particularly on Sundays.
>
> When you cannot go to a banquet, one of your friends often brings you a report of what took place, and tells you how much you were missed; often you are brought a piece of the cake, or a little portion of the banquet food; by these signs the community "reaches out" to make you one of them. In your parish something similar will take place. After Mass, someone will read a part of the Sunday scriptures to you, bring you the message of the homily and "your share" of the Lord's saving banquet, the Holy Eucharist.[17]

Father Michael Mathis, C.S.C., served as chaplain for twelve years at St. Joseph's Hospital in South Bend, Indiana. During that period this liturgical pioneer developed a unique "course of dying" based on an expectation of the Lord's coming. At the Worcester Liturgical Week in 1955, he described his use of the parables — the ten virgins (Matthew 28:1-13) and the watchful servants (Matthew 24:42-47) — to reach terminally ill patients. Pains and discomfort, in this approach, are viewed as the Lord "knocking." The question is: will the sick person be ready to open the door and welcome Christ when he comes? When Jesus does arrive he will take the sick person from all his misery and bring him to everlasting joy. Father Mathis goes on to say:

After this idea is deeply fixed in the mind and heart of a patient, then it will be easy to go on with the business of the immediate preparation for death. In fact, from now on everything will be easy, even if at times an embarrassing confession of sins has to be made. But equally important is the fact that the coming of Christ is an inspiring rallying point for the elusive consciousness of dying persons. Hence, so long as such a person is still conscious, without, however, overtaxing the waning strength of the patient, a chaplain, or a doctor, or a nurse, or a relative, can casually remark on seeing him still alive, "I see the Lord has not yet come." Invariably the sick person, who has been trained to expect really to see Jesus coming, will agree by word or by some expression that will indicate, usually with a smile, that he or she is waiting with joyful anticipation.[18]

Father Mathis calls dying "the great event" of a person's life; anointing the sick naturally should help the patient through this critical passage from here to eternity. But sometimes God delays his coming and wills the recovery of a sick person. The Lord often uses this sacrament as his instrument for healing. Priests in the ministry could recount countless incidents of that and some readers may have even experienced its marvelous restorative power in their own lives. A liturgical scholar in his discussion about public anointing of the sick cites this example to show the possible curative effect of communal prayer and sacramental anointment.

If a passing reminiscence is allowed, we should like to tell about an elderly lady who had requested the anointing before the community. We will call her Pauline. After she had received Communion, the others who were at Mass came in turn to the altar rail. As they were moving forward, a spontaneous, unrehearsed gesture began to take form: first, the women who were coming knelt there, and embraced her; then the men, after ever so slight a moment of hesitation, also paused at her side and took her hand . . . . Now, by the grace of God, the cancer which afflicted Pauline was retarded in its progress; she improved visibly and she went on for years more, a living vindication in that community of the sacrament of the anointing of the sick.[19]

B. The Funeral Liturgy

When fourth grader Judy Wilson died suddenly, the victim of an unusual disease, parishioners at Holy Family Church in Harrisburg, Pennsylvania, quickly came to the side of her grief-stricken family. There were messages of condolence and offers of help, but strongest support came in the evening at the funeral service. Judy's childish body was brought to the church in late afternoon and her parents began to receive callers at 6:00 P.M. in the vestibule. Around 7:30 a priest slipped into the confessional for the convenience of those who would participate in the Mass a half-hour later.

The liturgy itself spoke of hope, resurrection, eternal life. White vestments symbolized joy and victory; the paschal candle linked Judy's demise with baptism, Christ's triumph over death, and her ultimate sharing in Jesus' conquest; the biblical readings and other ritual texts expressed in words what these items said silently in sign. However, it probably was the congregation's presence and participation which most effectively lifted up the sorrowing mother, father, and family. United spoken responses, enthusiastic singing of victory hymns ("Let Hymns of Joy to Grief Succeed"), and common reception of our Risen Lord in the Eucharist made this body of worshipers one with the mourners and communicated strength to them. Faces told the story. Eyes wet with tears of anguish gradually changed and by the end of this funeral rite they quietly smiled with a serenity based on God's promise of an everlasting future.

The Harrisburg diocesan liturgical commission introduced this optional practice of evening funerals precisely to make possible in contemporary society the parish or community's participation in such farewell liturgies for the departed. An introductory catechesis to its guidelines gave doctrinal support for the innovation.

> In its renewal of the funeral rite the Church will be stressing the victorious character of Christian death through its selection of ceremonies, readings, prayers, music and color of vestments. True, we will always experience the need to lament and weep for our departed loved ones, as did Jesus. But it is surely appropriate that some time before burial the Christian *community* should *celebrate*, with some signs of joy, the "belief" that a brother or sister has entered the newness of eternal life. Otherwise it would be difficult to see how our affirmation of the resurrection could have any real or honest meaning.
>
> If our belief in resurrection has no way of being adequately expressed by the community on the occasion of death, of what "Christian" value is our sentimental tribute to the one who has fallen asleep in Christ? If friends and parishioners are limited to viewing a dead body, accompanied with some private devotions, are we not failing in giving full witness to our faith's most cherished belief at a time when witness could be most effective?[20]

These following practical points summarize Harrisburg's policy which facilitates a switch from the traditional and sparsely attended morning services to optional and more convenient evening funerals.

1. The evening funeral service is an option, left to the wishes of the deceased's family.

2. No evening funerals are to take place on Saturday or Sunday.

3. Burial would in most cases take place the next morning from the funeral parlor.

4. Viewing of the body may be held in the church lobby, a room or hall adjacent to the church, or in the church proper. A book for signing by visitors would be in order.

Any reservations a family has concerning the viewing should be respected.

5. "Flower cards," much like gift certificates, can be purchased from the florist and given to the parish. These will be redeemed for flowers at some future date for use in the church in memory of the deceased. This resolves in a practical way the legitimate desires of friends and the understandable anxiety of florists.

6. A priest should be available for confessions a half hour before time for the funeral Mass.

7. Some type of simple reception for the congregation afterwards in a parish hall is very desirable when circumstances permit.

8. The viewing in church is limited to one night. Priests may object that evening hours are always crowded with appointments. However, some of this time in the past has been spent in travel to funeral parlors for devotional prayers and calls of condolence. Moreover, the impact on many of a well attended, fully participated evening funeral rite and the great solace such a service supplies the mourning family would seem to outweigh any inconvenience this new arrangement causes parish priests.

A funeral rite (either the experimental form used in our country for the past several years or the revised one now ready), be it in the morning or evening, flows from faith and should foster hope. It also, however, serves as an opportunity for Christians to show how they love one another. The presence of so many parishioners at Judy Wilson's funeral reflected and expressed that kind of love for this little girl and her sorrowful parents. They were lending their support, manifesting their concern, offering their assistance. This sort of sympathy and understanding for the bereaved has a long tradition in mankind's history; the revised funeral rite builds on that custom and adds to it a renewed emphasis on the resurrection theme.

I remember some years ago reading, with great surprise and considerable disapproval, words by one of our most popular Catholic priest writers which seriously questioned the practice of "wakes." More specifically, he challenged the wisdom of priests traveling all over a city to spend ten minutes at the funeral parlor or read prayers at the cemetery. The author implied that this was a waste of time and inferred that clergymen could use these moments for better purposes. Doing what? Those critical hours in life, as we have suggested earlier, find men and women most responsive to the kindness, unconcern, or worse, harshness of others, especially the clergy. A priest in such instances can succeed admirably and never be forgotten, or fail miserably and never be forgiven.

The restored order for funerals seems to agree. Article 3 in its Introduction recommends a period for "waking" the body: "Between the time of death and burial there should be sufficient opportunities for the people to pray for the dead and profess their own faith in eternal life."[21] Later, in outlining the function of the priest on these occasions, it states he should "show loving concern for the family of the deceased person" and "support them in the time of sorrow."[22]

One hears occasionally an objection to the viewing of the body as a pagan practice which should be discontinued in our enlightened age. The official text takes a different approach. "The bodies of the faithful, which were temples of the Holy Spirit, should be shown honor and respect, but any kind of pomp and display should be avoided."[23] There are legitimate questions, of course. Should families feel constrained to select a casket and service too expensive for their means? Is the open bier pagan worship of the body or Christian reverence for the deceased? Would such viewing prove unbearable for the family or a consoling last look at their beloved? Does artificial grass over the mound of dirt next to a grave soften the blow or foster an escapist mentality? Do we drive home the impermanence of human life with that handful of sand ("Remember man that you are dust. . .") or do we, by this action, minimize our belief in the ultimate resurrection of a body about to be lowered into the earth? Are certain practices (e.g., hired cars for a longer procession, mammoth tombstones, artificial displays) designed to impress others or sincere signs of love?

These issues ought to be resolved according to this principle:

> In celebrating the funeral rites of their brothers and sisters, Christians should certainly affirm their hope of eternal life, but in such a way that they do not seem to neglect or ignore the feeling and practice of their own time and place. Family traditions, local customs, groups established to take care of funerals, anything that is good may be used freely, but anything alien to the Gospel should be changed so that funeral rites for Christians may proclaim the paschal faith and spirit of the Gospel.[24]

We can, therefore, rightfully wonder about certain excesses in practice or attitude, but the simple procedure of "calling hours" to pray for the dead and console the afflicted in itself appears sound and Christian. What kind of community prayer ought we to follow during these afternoon and evening sessions at the funeral parlor or family home? The rosary has long been the standby, but in recent years many have abandoned this devotion at "wakes" as lengthy, repetitious, and uncomfortable particularly when the room is crowded or mixed with many who are not Roman Catholic. Priests (or others when no clergyman is available) in its stead now often turn to some type of vigil or Bible service.

The revised norms for Christian burial certainly support this trend or preference.

> In celebrations for the dead, whether the funeral service or any other, emphasis should be given to the biblical readings. These proclaim the paschal mystery, support the hope of reunion in the kingdom of God, teach respect for the dead, and encourage the witness of Christian living.[25]

Green Bay's liturgical commission prepared "The Service of the Wake" as part of a package for the introduction of the experimental funeral rite. The "Leader's Book" contains a suggested procedure which includes an Our Father, Hail Mary, antiphonal recitation of psalms (129, 22, 114), scriptural readings (Apocalypse 21:2-5, 1 Thessalonians 4:13-18, John 16:20-22, John 11:21-27), a prayer of the faithful, several presidential prayers and a concluding hymn. Other dioceses and commercial publishers have also compiled similar biblical services for these occasions.

The efforts of both clergy and laity in comforting the mourners and praying for the deceased should continue long after the grave has been covered and the tombstone set. There usually will be visitors, cards, and flowers in abundance during those days immediately surrounding the death and burial. However, life moves on for all and in the months which follow the widow or widower, the saddened parents, the lonely survivor must face these realities pretty much on his or her own. An occasional visit or call, unexpected touches of thoughtfulness, can ease the ache and supply renewed hope.

Prayers for the dead express our belief in eternal life, our remembrance of one we loved, and our desire for the departed's everlasting peace. Without entering into the complicated issue of Mass stipends, we can assert that mention in eucharistic services of those who have died still represents the highest form of intercession on their behalf. Revisions in the Church calendar open so many weekdays for optional celebrations that one could view this as an invitation to reintroduce the frequent "black" Masses of a previous age. The General Instruction indicates otherwise, and explains why. "For similar reasons the Mass for the dead should be used sparingly. Every Mass is offered for both the living and the dead, and there is a remembrance of the dead in each eucharistic prayer."[26]

The revised rite for funerals from Rome with adaptations to fit cultural conditions of the United States seeks in a variety of ways to communicate the true meaning of Jesus' paschal mystery in the context of a Christian's death. A listing of salient features in this renewed service with an explanation of the what and the why behind them should illustrate how it accomplishes this.

The present volume has taken as its starting point the official flexibility in liturgical texts published by the Holy See as a response to the directives of the Constitution on the Sacred Liturgy. Each of the restored ritual books (e.g., baptism and marriage) includes, as we have seen, a rich selection of scriptural readings, prayers, and blessings, together with other options. The rite for funerals is no exception. It contains in the original Latin edition (without additional alternatives or any adjustments introduced by the National Conference of Catholic Bishops in the United States) over forty biblical passages, nearly twenty psalms, and a host of prayer formulas to fit varying situations. The presumption here is that the celebrant working in sympathetic and close cooperation with the bereaved family will choose those which seem most appropriate for the circumstances. Introductory guidelines in the official text make this point very specifically.

> In preparing and arranging funeral celebrations priests should consider the deceased and the circumstance of his life and death and be concerned also for the sorrow of the relatives and their Christian needs. Priests should be especially aware of persons, Catholic or non-Catholic, who seldom or never participate in the eucharist or who seem to have lost their faith, but who assist at liturgical celebrations and hear the Gospel on the occasion of funerals. Priests must remember that they are ministers of Christ's Gospel to all men.[27]

Among other things, the priest should:

1. Visit the sick and the dying, as indicated in the relevant section of the Roman Ritual.
2. Teach the significance of Christian death.
3. Show loving concern for the family of the deceased person, support them in the time of sorrow, and, as much as possible, involve them in planning the funeral celebration and the choice of the options made available in the rite.
4. Integrate the liturgy for the dead with the whole parish liturgical life and the pastoral ministry.[28]

Black and, more recently, purple have been customary vestment colors for the requiem Mass and funeral service. The revised rites' Introduction permits episcopal conferences to determine the liturgical color "in accordance with popular feeling. The color should not be offensive to human sorrow but should express Christian hope enlightened by the paschal mystery."[29] The American bishops in November, 1969, made optional white vestments, symbolic not necessarily of the departed's innocence, but of his hoped-for-rising to a glorious life. This has, in fact, through use of the experimental text, become rather common in the United States.

The large paschal candle, carried in procession and placed near the casket, links together an entire network of related notions—baptism, the resurrection, Easter, and, of course, entrance into eternal bliss. So, too, a Bible or cross placed on the coffin or a white resurrection cloth (which recalls the baptismal garment) draped over the casket speaks of a future life for the dead Christian.

The service in church immediately after Mass, once termed absolution, has been changed to a ritual of final commendation. "This rite is not to be understood as a purification of the dead—which is effected rather by the eucharistic sacrifice—but as the last farewell with which the Christian community honors one of its members before the body is buried. Although in death there is a certain separation, Christians, who are members of Christ and are in him, can never be really separated by death."[30]

This introduction (others are given as alternatives) to the rite of farewell or commendation captures the spirit of that ceremony:

> With faith in Jesus Christ,
>> we reverently bring the body of our brother (sister)
>> to be buried in its human imperfection.
> Let us pray with confidence to God,
>> who gives life to all things,
>> that he will raise up this mortal body
>> to the perfection and the company of the saints.

> May God give him (her) a merciful judgment
>   and forgive all his (her) sins.
> May Christ, the Good Shepherd,
>   lead him (her) safely home
>   to be at peace with God our Father.
> And may he (she) be happy for ever
>   with all the saints
>   in the presence of the eternal King.[31]

After a prayer in silence, some words of greeting by relatives of the deceased (if desired), sprinkling with holy water, and the incensation of the body, the celebrant concludes with this farewell prayer (or an alternative one):

> Father,
>   into your hands we commend our brother (sister).
> We are confident that with all who have died in Christ
>   he (she) will be raised to life on the last day
>   and live with Christ forever.
> (We thank you for all the blessings
>   you gave him (her) in this life
>   to show your fatherly care for all of us
>   and the fellowship which is ours with the saints
>   in Jesus Christ.)
>
> Lord, hear our prayer:
>   welcome our brother (sister) to paradise
>   and help us to comfort each other
>   with the assurance of our faith
>   (until we all meet in Christ
>   to be with you and with our brother (sister) for
>   ever).
> (We ask this) through Christ our Lord.
> Amen.[32]

The Roman document offers this explanation of holy water and incense in the funeral rite. "The sprinkling with holy water, which recalls the person's entrance into eternal life through baptism, and the incensation, which honors the body of the deceased as temple of the Holy Spirit, may also be considered signs of farewell."[33]

Cremation has generally been prohibited by the Church as a procedure which questioned belief in the resurrection of the dead and diminished respect for the departed. Today's population explosion and problems of space connected with the world's growth, however, alters that picture. New directives state: "Christian funeral rites are permitted for those who choose to have their bodies cremated unless it is shown that they have acted for reasons contrary to Christian principles."[34] At the same time, the document stresses that when cremation is employed, these funeral rites should be celebrated in such a way "that does not hide the Church's preference for the custom of burying the dead in a grave or tomb, as the Lord himself willed to be buried."[35]

Those final moments before a body is lowered into its resting spot at the cemetery are exceedingly difficult ones for mourners. In past years family and friends stood rather silently, except for a recited Our Father or several hesitant "Amens," while the priest read from his ritual. The revised ceremony provides for more active involvement upon the part of those who travel to the graveside for the actual burial. The initial prayer offered as the body is being placed in the grave or tomb continues a theme of commendation or farewell and couples with it the ever-present notions of faith and hope.

> Since almighty God has called our brother (sister) N.
>   from this life to himself,
>   we commit his (her) body
>   to the earth from which it was made.
>
> Christ was the first to rise from the dead,
>   and we know that he will raise up our mortal bodies
>   to be like his in glory.
>
> We commend our brother (sister) to the Lord:
>   may the Lord receive him (her) in his peace
>   and raise up his (her) body on the last day.[36]

This Prayer of the Faithful, or one similar to it, follows:

> Let us pray for our brother (sister)
>   to our Lord Jesus Christ, who said:

"I am the resurrection and the life.
The man who believes in me will live
  even if he dies,
  and every person
  who puts his faith in me
  will never suffer eternal death."

Lord, you wept at the death of Lazarus, your friend:
  comfort us in our sorrow.
  We ask this in faith:
     Response: Lord, hear our prayer.

You raised the dead to life:
  give your brother (sister) eternal life.
  We ask this in faith:
     Lord, hear our prayer.

You promised paradise to the thief who repented:
  bring our brother (sister) to the joys of heaven.
  We ask this in faith:
     Lord, hear our prayer.

Our brother (sister) was washed clean in baptism
  and anointed with the oil of salvation:
  give him (her) fellowship with all your saints.
  We ask this in faith:
     Lord, hear our prayer.

He (she) was nourished with your body and blood:
  grant him (her) a place at the table in your heavenly
    kingdom.
  We ask this in faith:
     Lord, hear our prayer.

Comfort us in our sorrow at the death of our brother
    (sister):
  let our faith be our consolation
  and eternal life our hope.
  We ask this in faith:
     Lord, hear our prayer.[37]

Afterwards all recite the Lord's Prayer, listen to the celebrant's concluding oration, and "at the end of the entire rite, an

appropriate song may be sung, according to local custom."[38] This last suggestion may seem unusual and impractical in our environment. Nevertheless, I did hear of an instance last year in which, at the interment of a young priest, the great crowd of mourners sang "To Jesus Christ Our Sovereign King" with strength and conviction as their final salute to this brother Christian. Those final phrases, "Christ Jesus Victor, Christ Jesus Ruler, Christ Jesus Lord and Redeemer," echoed across the cemetery and announced to the world what is the basis for our belief in eternal life.

The revised ritual for funerals also encourages a brief homily (not a eulogy) at the standard time in Mass (not after the eucharistic celebration). It also supplies a special series of prayers for the burial of baptized and unbaptized infants. Finally, it provides a number of orations to cover special circumstances: "For a young person, for one who worked in the service of the gospel, for one who suffered a long illness, for one who died suddenly, for parents, for a married couple."[39]

I think the opening words of this restored funeral ritual quoted below bring to a fitting conclusion the present chapter and this entire book. Christ's paschal mystery dominates both. That fundamental truth forms the foundation for our hope at death, the reason we gather at altars for the Eucharist, the motive for liturgical celebrations of every kind. Jesus is truly present in mystery through faith at our liturgies; he will be there in fullness face to face at our deaths. These lines say it all:

In the funeral rites the Church celebrates the paschal mystery of Christ. Those who in baptism have become one with the dead and risen Christ will pass with him from death to life, to be purified in soul and welcomed into the fellowship of the saints in heaven. They look forward in blessed hope to his second coming and the bodily resurrection of the dead.[40]

Notes

Introduction

1. *General Instruction* to the *Roman Missal.* Translated by International Committee on English in the Liturgy, Inc. Toronto, Canada, 1969, article 6.

2. Pope Paul VI, "Changes in the Mass." An Address given on November 19, 1969. Cf. *Newsletter*, Bishops' Committee on the Liturgy, January, 1970, p. 3.

3. *General Instruction, op. cit.,* article 58.

Part I   The Celebrant's Attitude in a Flexible Liturgy

Chapter 1   Master of the Situation

1. O'Connell, J. *The Celebration of Mass.* Milwaukee: Bruce, 1941, pp. 285–286.

2. St. Pius X, Motu Proprio *Tra le sollecitudini*, November 22, 1903, on the "Restoration of Sacred Music." From *The Liturgy.* Boston: Daughters of St. Paul, 1962, p. 178.

3. *Documents of Vatican II*. Walter M. Abbott, S.J., General Editor. New York: The America Press, 1966. Constitution on the Sacred Liturgy, article 30.

4. Broccolo, Gerard. "Basic Suppositions of Liturgical Change." Chicago: Liturgy Training Program, 1969, p. 8.

5. *General Instruction, op. cit.*, article 313.

6. *Documents of Vatican II, op. cit.*, article 11.

Chapter 2   Man of Prayer

1. *General Instruction, op. cit.*, article 60.

2. *The Order of Mass.* Translated by the International Committee on English in the Liturgy, Inc. Toronto, Canada, 1969, number 6.

3. Greeley, A. *New Horizons for the Priesthood.* New York: Sheed and Ward, 1970, p. 137.

4. *Ibid.*, p. 138.

Chapter 3   Faith and Commitment

1. "The Place of Music in Eucharistic Celebrations." A Statement by the Bishops' Committee on the Liturgy. Washington: United States Catholic Conference Publications Office, 1968.

Chapter 4   Presence of Christ

1. *Documents of Vatican II, op. cit.*, article 7.

2. Roguet, A. M. *Christ Acts through the Sacraments.* Translated by Carisbrooke Dominicans. Collegeville, Minnesota: The Liturgical Press, 1961.

3. Küng, Hans. *The Church.* New York: Sheed and Ward, 1967, p. 235.

Chapter 5   Shepherd, Preacher, Celebrant

1. Sigur, Alexander. "Today's Priest—GP or More?" *America*, March 7, 1970, pp. 237–238.

2. Bianchi, Eugene. "How Quitters Can Be Reformers." *National Catholic Reporter*, May 8, 1970.

3. Sigur, *op. cit.*

4. Greeley, *op. cit.*, p. 143.

5. Letters to the Editor. *America*, March 28, 1970, pp. 320–322.

6. *Ibid.*, p. 322.

7. Kasper, Walter. "A New Dogmatic Outlook on the Priestly Ministry," in *The Pastoral Identity of the Priest*, edited by Karl Rahner, S. J. Concilium Vol. 43. New York: Paulist Press, 1969, p. 27.

8. *Documents of Vatican II*, *op. cit.*, "Dogmatic Constitution on the Church," article 28.

Chapter 6 Leader of Christian Worship

1. Suenens, Léon-Joseph Cardinal. *Co-Responsibility in the Church*. Translated by Francis Martin. New York: Herder and Herder, 1968, p. 113.

2. Küng, *op. cit.*, p. 235.

3. *Documents of Vatican II*, *op. cit.*, "Constitution on the Sacred Liturgy," article 41.

4. Jungmann, Joseph A., S.J. *The Mass of the Roman Rite*. Translated by Rev. Francis A. Brunner, C.SS.R. New York: Benziger Bros., Inc., 1959, p. 147–148.

5. *Documents of Vatican II*, *op. cit.*, "Constitution on the Sacred Liturgy," article 42.

6. *Ibid.*, article 43.

Chapter 7 A Healthy Regard for Rubrics

1. Noldin, H., S.J., and Schmitt, A., S.J. *Summa Theologiae Moralis*. Barcelona: Herder, 1951, Vol. III, p. 25.

2. *General Instruction*, *op. cit.*, article 6.

3. *Ibid.*, article 5.

4. *Documents of Vatican II*, *op. cit.*, "Constitution on the Sacred Liturgy," article 23.

5. Pope Paul VI, Apostolic Constitution, "Promulgation of the Roman Missal Restored by Decree of the Second Vatican Ecumenical Council," April 3, 1969.

Chapter 8   Relaxed and Natural

1. Hovda, Robert. "Style and Presence in Celebration." *Worship*, November, 1967, pp. 514–522.

2. *Ibid.*, p. 521.

3. Milwaukee Archdiocesan Liturgical Commission. "The Role of the Celebrant in a Flexible Liturgy." January, 1970.

4. Hovda, *op. cit.*, p. 520, 521.

5. Hovda, Robert. "Presidency and Ministry — A Style of Celebration." *Living Worship*, May, 1966.

Chapter 9   President of the Community

1. *General Instruction*, *op. cit.*, article 7.

2. *Ibid.*, article 271.

3. *Ibid.*, article 62.

4. Boyer, Louis, *Liturgical Piety*. Notre Dame: University of Notre Dame Press, 1954, p. 24.

5. *Ibid.*, p. 29

6. Hitchcock, James. "Here Lies Community: R.I.P." *America*, May 30, 1970, p. 581.

7. *Ibid.*, p. 580.

8. *Ibid.*, p. 581.

9. *General Instruction*, *op. cit.*, article 75.

10. *Ibid.*, article 24.

11. *Ibid.*, article 20.

12. *Ibid.*, article 56.

13. *Ibid.*, articles 11, 10, 13.

14. *Priest's Guide to Parish Worship.* Washington: The Liturgical Conference, 1964, pp. 29–30.

15. *Ibid.*, p. 30.

16. *General Instruction, op. cit.*, article 2.

Chapter 10   Communication I — Reading

1. Hovda, "Style and Presence in Celebration," *op. cit.*, p. 517.

2. *General Instruction, op. cit.*, article 66.

3. *Ibid.*, article 18.

4. *Ibid.*, article 33.

5. *Ibid.*, article 34.

6. *Ibid.*, article 35.

7. *Ibid.*, article 66.

8. *Ibid.*, article 66.

9. *Newsletter*, Bishops' Committee on the Liturgy, October, 1968; December, 1969.

10. Wesley, Robert J. "A Study of Instruction for Liturgical Reading in Roman Catholic Seminaries in the United States." Unpublished dissertation for a doctor of philosophy degree at Wayne State University, 1969.

11. Clarke, Raymond. *Sounds Effective.* London: Geoffrey Chapman, 1969, pp. 50–53.

12. Küng, *op. cit.*, p. 235.

13. Clarke, *op. cit.*, pp. 37–39.

14. *Newsletter*, Bishops' Commission on the Liturgical Apostolate, December, 1965.

15. Clarke, *op. cit.*, p. 50.

16. *Ibid.*, p. 52.

Chapter 11   Communication II — Preaching

1. Curran, Charles A. "Personal Change Through Sermons." *Guide*, January 1964, pp. 3–10.

2. *Ibid.*, p. 4.

3. *Ibid.*, p. 8.

4. *Instruction for the Proper Implementation of the Constitution on the Sacred Liturgy*, September 26, 1964, article 54.

5. *General Instruction, op. cit.*, article 41.

6. "Hugh Hefner Faces Middle Age." *Time*, February 14, 1969, pp. 69–70.

7. Curran, *op. cit.*, p. 8.

8. Clarke, *op. cit.*, p. 31.

9. *A Handbook for the Revised Roman Liturgy*. Prepared and published by the Diocesan Liturgical Commissions of New York, Brooklyn, and Rockville Centre. January, 1970, pp. 22–24.

Chapter 12   Communication III — Proclaiming

1. Harrison, G.B. "Englishing the New Liturgy." *America*, May 9, 1970, p. 495.

2. Brusselman, Christiane. "Prayer — The Need We Feel." Talk given at the Atlanta Congress on Worship, April 17, 1970. Transcribed by Sister Janice Risse, M.S.B.T., with excerpt printed in *Liturgy*, newsletter of Mobile Liturgical Commission.

3. *Newsletter*, Bishops' Commission on the Liturgical Apostolate, December, 1965.

4. *General Instruction, op. cit.*, article 12.

5. *Ibid.*, article 14.

6. *Documents of Vatican II, op. cit.*, "Constitution on the Sacred Liturgy," article 21.

7. *Ibid.*, article 34.

8. *General Instruction, op. cit.*, article 24.

9. *Ibid.*, article 25.

10. *Ibid.*, article 28.

11. *Ibid.*, article 32.

12. *Ibid.*, article 32.

13. *Ibid.*, article 49.

14. Hovda, Robert. *Manual of Celebration.* Washington: The Liturgical Conference, 1970, Mass/21.

15. *General Instruction, op. cit.*, article 55.

16. *The Order of Mass, op. cit.*, numbers 19 and 21.

17. *Ibid.*, number 27.

18. Bishops' Committee on the Liturgy. *The New Eucharistic Prayers and Prefaces.* Washington: National Conference of Catholic Bishops, 1968, p. 20.

19. "The Place of Music in Eucharistic Celebrations," *op. cit.*, p. 4.

20. *The Order of Mass, op. cit.*, numbers 62–63.

21. *General Instruction, op. cit.*, article 56.

22. *The Order of Mass, op. cit.*, number 100.

23. *General Instruction, op. cit.*, article 56.

24. *Ibid.*, article 283.

25. Clarke, *op. cit.*, p. 33.

26. *General Instruction, op. cit.*, article 55.

27. *The Order of Mass, op. cit.*, number 113.

Chapter 13   Planning the Liturgy

1. *General Instruction, op. cit.*, article 3.

2. *Ibid.*, article 5.

3. *Ibid.*, article 73.

4. *Ibid.*, article 313.

5. *Ibid.*, article 316.

6. *Documents of Vatican II, op. cit.,* "Constitution on the Sacred Liturgy," article 11.

7. *Ibid.*, article 29.

8. *Ibid.*, article 10.

9. *Ibid.*

10. *Ibid.*

11. *General Instruction, op. cit.,* article 1.

12. *Ibid.*

Part 2   Worship at the Major Moments of Life

Chapter 1   The Parish Worship Committee

1. Hovda, *Manual of Celebration*, Introduction, pp. 18–20.

2. Chicago, Baltimore, Denver, Cincinnati, Lansing, Richmond, Green Bay, Joliet.

3. *Parish Liturgy Team.* Liturgical Training Program, 5947 N. Manton Ave., Chicago, Illinois 60646, p. 12.

4. 1 Corinthians 13:1.

5. *Documents of Vatican II, op. cit.,* "Constitution on the Sacred Liturgy," article 7.

6. Winter, Art. "How Goes Church Reform?" *National Catholic Reporter*, August 7, 1970.

7. *Newsletter*, Bishops' Committee on the Liturgy, December, 1969.

8. *Lectionary for Mass.* United States Catholic Conference, 1312 Massachusetts Avenue, N.W., Washington, D.C., 20005.

9. For a development of these ideas consult the April, 1970 issue of *Living Worship*, "Themes for Celebration — Successor to the Calendar?"

10. "The Place of Music in Eucharistic Celebrations," *op. cit.*; Bauman, William A. "The New Mass — Challenge to the Creative Musician," NCMEA *Overtones*, December, 1969. NCMEA National Office, 4637 Eastern Avenue, N.E., Washington, D.C. 20018.

Chapter 2   Born Again

1. *Documents· of Vatican II, op. cit.,* "Constitution on the Sacred Liturgy," articles 66–70.

2. *Rite of Baptism for Children.* Translated by International Committee on English in the Liturgy, Inc. Toronto, Canada, 1970. "Christian Initiation," article 2.

3. *Ibid.,* "Baptism of Children," no. 5.

4. *Ibid.,* no. 5(2).

5. *Ibid.,* no. 5(3).

6. *Ibid.,* no. 5(5).

7. *Ibid.,* "Christian Initiation," article 3.

8. *Ibid.,* "Baptism of Children," no. 2.

9. *Ibid.,* no. 3.

10. *Ibid.,* no. 77.

11. *Ibid.,* "Christian Initiation," article 4.

12. *Ibid.,* article 7.

13. *Ibid.,* "Baptism of Children," no. 4.

14. *Ibid.,* no. 70a.

15. *Ibid.,* no. 79.

16. *Ibid.*, "Christian Initiation," articles 18–20.

17. *Ibid.*, article 21.

18. *Ibid.*, article 22.

19. *Ibid.*, article 6.

20. *Ibid.*, "Baptism of Children," no. 100.

21. *Ibid.*, no. 68.

22. *Ibid.*, no. 9.

23. *Ibid.*, no. 29.

24. *Collectio Rituum.* Ritual approved by the National Conference of Bishops of the United States of America. New York: Benziger Brothers, 1964. "The Rite for the Baptism of More than One Child," numbers 3, 5, 7.

25. *Rite of Baptism for Children, op. cit.,* "Baptism of Children," no. 49b.

26. *Ibid.*, no. 248.

27. *Ibid.*, no. 70a.

28. *Ibid.*, "Christian Initiation," article 27.

29. *Ibid.*, "Baptism of Children," no. 9.

30. *Ibid.*, no. 7(1).

31. *Ibid.*, no. 7(2).

32. *Ibid.*, no. 5(1).

33. *Ibid.*, "Christian Initiation," article 15.

34. *Ibid.*, article 33.

35. *Ibid.*, "Baptism of Children," no. 10.

36. Champlin, Joseph M. "The Light of Christ." A leaflet to accompany the baptismal candle reprinted from an article in the August, 1970 *Homiletic and Pastoral Review.* Will and Baumer Candle Company, Syracuse, New York 13201.

Chapter 3   To Love and Honor Each Other All the Days of Our Lives

1. Von Hoffman, Nicholas. "Divorcing Marriage." Washington *Post*, June 5, 1970, pp. Bl, B4.

2. Champlin, Charles. "A Mess of Movies Look at the Mess of Marriage." Los Angeles *Times*, May 10, 1970, Calendar section, pp. 1, 12.

3. "Theology of Marriage" appeared in original form as part of a filmstrip kit, *Together for Life*, written by this writer and produced by Alpha Corporation of America, Elk Grove Village, Illinois, August, 1970.

4. Hosea 2:22–24.

5. Jeremiah 3.

6. Ezekiel 16:59–63.

7. Isaiah 54:5–6.

8. Exodus 24:3–8.

9. *Ibid.*, 19:8.

10. *Documents of Vatican II, op, cit.*, "Dogmatic Constitution on the Church," article 11.

11. *Ibid.*, "Decree on the Apostolate of the Laity," article 11.

12. Champlin, Joseph M. *Together for Life*. Notre Dame, Indiana: Ave Maria Press, 1970, both paperback and booklet editions.

13. *Together for Life* Filmstrip, *op. cit.*

14. Champlin, Joseph M. *Together for Life*, pp. 64, 66.

15. *Ibid.*, pp. 65, 67.

Chapter 4   A Change of Heart and Peace

1. Corrigan, John E. "Bless Me, Father." Chicago: Claretian Publications, 1967, pp. 12–13.

2. Report, June 8, 1970, on Penance Survey conducted by Rev. James Sullivan, chairman of the Lansing liturgy committee, for the Federation of Diocesan Liturgical Commissions.

3. Results of questionnaire on auricular confession submitted in July 1970 to parish priests by the Grand Rapids Diocesan Liturgical Commission.

4. Kavanagh, Aidan, O.S.B. "The Purpose of Christian Penance." A conference on "The Liturgy of Christian Penance" sponsored by the Graduate Program in Liturgical Studies at Notre Dame, June 9–12, 1970.

5. Riga, Peter. *Sin and Penance.* Milwaukee: Bruce, 1961, pp. 70–73.

6. Acts of the Apostles 20:31.

7. *Documents of Vatican II*, *op. cit.*, "Dogmatic Constitution on the Church," article 11.

8. Bausch, William J. *It Is the Lord!* Notre Dame, Indiana: Fides, 1970, p. 94.

9. Quinn, John J. "The Lord's Supper and Forgiveness of Sin." *Worship*, May, 1968, p. 281.

10. *New Saint Joseph Sunday Missal and Hymnal.* New York: Catholic Book Publishing Co., 1970.

11. Quinn, *op. cit.*, pp. 290–291.

12. *Ibid.*, p. 291.

13. *Documents of Vatican II*, *op. cit.*, "Constitution on the Sacred Liturgy," article 27.

14. Foley, Leonard, O.F.M. *What's Happening to Confession?* Cincinnati: St. Anthony Messenger Press, 1970, p. 62.

15. Corrigan, John E. "Penance: A Service to the Community," in *Worship in the City of Man*, Twenty-Seventh North American Liturgical Week, Houston, Texas, August 22–25, 1966. Published by the Liturgical Conference, Washington, D. C., 1966, pp. 109–110.

16. *Ibid.*, pp. 110–111.

17. "Public Celebration of Penance: A Pastoral Letter of the Bishops of Holland," *Worship*, May, 1966, p. 280.

18. "The Sacrament of Reconciliation." Guidelines and Directives for the Celebration of a Communal Penance Service issued June 13, 1969 by the Madison Diocesan Liturgical Commission.

19. *The Book of Catholic Worship*. Washington: The Liturgical Conference, 1966, pp. 736–745; Foley, *op. cit.*, pp. 99–111; Haring, Bernard. *Shalom*: *The Sacrament of Peace*. New York: Farrar, Straus and Giroux, 1968, pp. 301–302; Hoey, Robert F. *The Experimental Liturgy Book*. New York: Herder and Herder, 1969, pp. 178–185.

20. Longley, Alfred C. *Healing and Forgiveness*. Cincinnati: World Library of Sacred Music, 1967.

21. Three extensive articles, "The Sacrament of Penance Today," by Rev. Charles E. Curran which appeared in *Worship*, November and December, 1969 and January, 1970, contain an excellent survey of the sacrament's historical, theological, and pastoral aspects.

22. Gordon, Noah. *The Rabbi*. New York: Fawcett World Library, 1965, p. 179.

23. Foley, Leonard, O.F.M. "What Do You Mean, 'Teach', Religion?" *St. Anthony Messenger*, September, 1970, p. 21.

24. Corrigan, John E. "Bless Me, Father," *op. cit.*

25. Foley, *What's Happening to Confession*? pp. 113–117.

26. *The Book of Catholic Worship.*, *op. cit.*, pp 741–742.

27. McManus, Frederick R. "The Roman Reform of the Liturgy of Penance." A lecture at the Notre Dame Conference, "The Liturgy of Christian Penance," *op. cit.*, June 12, 1970.

28. *Ibid.*

Chapter 5   On Dying, Death, and Rising

1. *Documents of Vatican II*, *op. cit.*, "Constitution on the Sacred Liturgy," article 47.

2. *Ibid.*, article 6.

3. *Roman Calendar.* Translated by International Committee on English in the Liturgy, Inc. Toronto, Canada, pp. 7–8, article 4.

4. *Ibid*, p. 10, article 18.

5. *Ibid.*, p. 10, article 22.

6. Bishops' Committee on the Liturgy. *The New Eucharistic Prayers and Prefaces, op. cit.,* p. 51.

7. *Ibid.*, p. 45.

8. Matthew 9:35.

9. Luke 9:1.

10. Mark 6:12–13.

11. James 5:14–17.

12. *Documents of Vatican II, op. cit.,* "Constitution on the Sacred Liturgy," articles 73–74.

13. *Sources of Christian Theology,* Volume II, *Sacraments and Forgiveness.* Edited with commentary by Paul F. Palmer, S. J. Westminster, Maryland: The Newman Press, 1959, pp. 273–320. This is an invaluable source treatment of the history and doctrinal development of extreme unction.

14. "The Sacrament for the Anointing of the Sick." A translation from the Latin and French of an article in *Notitiae,* January, 1970, number 50, pp. 13–33 by Rev. Michael J. Mc-Manus and Sister Simone Begin, F.C.S.P. Available from the National Association of Catholic Chaplains, 1312 Massachusetts Avenue, N. W., Washington, D. C. 20005.

15. National Association of Catholic Chaplains. *Newsletter,* May, 1970. Executive Secretary, 1312 Massachusetts Avenue, N. W., Washington, D. C. 20005.

16. *Fear Not I Am With You.* Prepared by the National Association of Catholic Chaplains. New York: Joseph F. Wagner, Inc., and Alba House, 1970.

17. Episcopal letter to the sick issued by the Belgian hierarchy, 1970. Cf. *Service du Seigneur*, fevrier, 1970, n. 3, pp. 14–16. Unofficial translation by the Canadian National Liturgical Office, Ottawa.

18. Mathis, Michael, C.S.C. "Preparing for Death," in *The New Ritual Liturgy and Social Order*, Sixteenth National Liturgical Week, Worcester, Massachusetts, 1955. Published by the Liturgical Conference, Elsberry, Missouri, 1956, p. 47.

19. Heuschen, Louis, "The Sacraments and Care of Souls," in *The Liturgy of Vatican II*, edited by William Barauna, O.F.M., Volume II. Chicago: Franciscan Herald Press, 1966, p. 158.

20. "Guidelines for Evening Funerals." Harrisburg Diocesan Liturgical Commission, October, 1969.

21. *The Rite of Funerals*. Translation by the International Committee on English in the Liturgy, Inc. Toronto, Canada, 1970, article 3.

22. *Ibid.*, article 25.

23. *Ibid.*, article 3.

24. *Ibid.*, article 2.

25. *Ibid.*, article 11.

26. *General Instruction*, *op. cit.*, article 316.

27. *The Rite of Funerals*, *op. cit.*, article 18.

28. *Ibid.*, article 25.

29. *Ibid.*, article 22, no. 6.

30. *Ibid.*, article 10.

31. *Ibid.*, number 46.

32. *Ibid.*, number 48.

33. *Ibid.*, article 10.

34. *Ibid.*, article 15.

35. *Ibid.*

36. *Ibid.*, number 55.

37. *Ibid.*, number 56.

38. *Ibid.*, number 57.

39. *Ibid.*, numbers 177–182.

40. *Ibid.*, article 1.